Workplace Wellbeing

Workplace Wellbeing: A Relational Approach presents the most important, insightful, and up-to-date academic thinking and research related to flourishing at work. It also describes the transformative humanistic skills, values, and attributes ordinarily adopted by counsellors and psychotherapists alike, and shows how they may be transferred from a therapeutic setting to the workplace. Integrating ideas and strategies from counselling and psychotherapy, the book gathers together a wealth of accessible, interactive exercises and resources to help develop the skills and personal awareness to thrive in organisations.

Workplace Wellbeing: A Relational Approach examines how we can create an emotionally healthy workplace for all of us. It will prove useful for counsellors and psychotherapists alike, whether in training or practice in an organisational setting. More importantly, however, it is designed to be of value to the non-specialist, particularly those working in business, education, healthcare, human resources, occupational health, and organisational psychology.

James Costello is Senior Lecturer in Counselling and Psychotherapy at the University of the West of England, a Registered Accredited Member of the British Association for Counselling and Psychotherapy, and a BACP Senior Accredited Supervisor. His experience as a therapist and supervisor comes from practice across the private, third, and public sectors. Originally trained as a research scientist working in industry and academia, he believes that flourishing, innovation, and learning are all social processes with the transformative power of relationships at their heart. An experienced trade union case worker, he successfully applies a Relational Approach to training, supervision, advocacy, conflict resolution, and mediation across a range of workplace settings.

Workplace Wellbeing

A Relational Approach

James Costello

Routledge
Taylor & Francis Group

LONDON AND NEW YORK

First published 2020
by Routledge
2 Park Square, Milton Park, Abingdon, Oxon OX14 4RN

and by Routledge
52 Vanderbilt Avenue, New York, NY 10017

Routledge is an imprint of the Taylor & Francis Group, an informa business

© 2020 James Costello

British Library Cataloguing-in-Publication Data
A catalogue record for this book is available from the British Library

Library of Congress Cataloging-in-Publication Data
Names: Costello, James F. (James Francis), author.
Title: Workplace wellbeing : a relational approach / James Costello.
Description: Abingdon, Oxon ; New York, NY : Routledge, 2020. |
Includes bibliographical references and index.
Identifiers: LCCN 2020014108 (print) | LCCN 2020014109 (ebook) |
ISBN 9781138605305 (hardback) | ISBN 9781138605312 (paperback) |
ISBN 9780429468186 (ebook)
Subjects: LCSH: Job stress. | Employees–Mental health. |
Quality of work life–Psychological aspects. |
Industrial psychiatry. | Psychology, Industrial.
Classification: LCC HF5548.85 .C675 2020 (print) |
LCC HF5548.85 (ebook) | DDC 158.7/2–dc23
LC record available at https://lccn.loc.gov/2020014108
LC ebook record available at https://lccn.loc.gov/2020014109

ISBN: 978-1-138-60530-5 (hbk)
ISBN: 978-1-138-60531-2 (pbk)
ISBN: 978-0-429-46818-6 (ebk)

Typeset in Bembo
by Newgen Publishing UK

For Sonia my wife & our daughters
Evelyn & Isabella

Contents

List of boxes

Case studies

Reflective exercises

Skills exercises

Information

Acknowledgements

I have enjoyed an uncommon degree of professional and personal development during my time at the University of the West of England, joining as a Chemist and moving over time into the discipline of Psychotherapy. I am fortunate that my colleagues share with me the view that if teachers do not model what it is to grow and thrive, then what *do* we offer? I am indebted then to the management team, past and present, here in the Department of Applied Sciences (Lucy Meredith, Lyn Newton, Antony Hill, Sarah Bateman, and Helen Green) for both their support and courage to experiment. Thanks also to Kevin Honeychurch with whom I have shared an office during the writing of this book, both for his forbearance, and insights into Michels' Iron Law.

I am also fortunate to have worked for the University and College Union (UCU) for many years as an elected executive member of my local branch, and a caseworker specialising in wellbeing. Representing our members at both local and national levels has been an illuminating experience, and in many ways their stories have inspired this book. It has been humbling to be alongside principled and energetic activists who work tirelessly to build a fairer and more humane workplace for all employees to enjoy. Countless others, unionised and otherwise from across many organisations, have supported me in this project, although Andy Tubb (UCU) and Dave Pomroy (Unison) have been especially generous with their time, insights, and good humour. I have also learnt a great deal from working alongside various health and safety (H&S) and human resources (HR) professionals equally committed to creating a workplace in which we can all thrive.

My special thanks extend to colleagues in the counselling and psychotherapy profession who are a constant source of warmth, inspiration, and support. At UWE I have the good fortune to work alongside Alison Rouse, Dani Sinclair, Nigel Williams, Niki Gibbs, and the ever-cheerful Wayne Gardner, who is also consultant for my supervision practice. Also, Donal Carmody, who divides his time between UWE and managing *Kinergy*, and Kerry Evans, my inspirational supervisor there. I am especially indebted to my esteemed colleagues Liz

Maliphant, leader of the MA in Counselling and Psychotherapy at UWE, and Peter Lowis of the Bath Centre for Psychotherapy, who provided invaluable feedback on early drafts of chapters about attachment and groups, respectively. I am also indebted to Kieran Kelly who read early drafts of each chapter; as an experienced executive coach, I found his no-nonsense approach to nonsense invaluable. And to Phil Martin, who taught me that we can also do well outside organisations.

The experience of working in public-sector staff counselling services shaped how I think about workplace wellbeing. Although I felt I was helping, there was always something palliative about supporting people endure an emotionally harmful working environment. We can do better than this. The experience of my clients helped me recognise the need to go beyond the consulting room, and move further upstream to try and prevent people from tumbling into the broiling torrent in the first place. I would further like to thank those who attend my courses on *Workplace Wellbeing*, for their openness, their feedback about the experiential exercises and course content that form the core of this book, and most importantly their encouragement to keep on going.

Carrie Rhys-Davies has done far more than illustrate the book. Working alongside her has been an immensely enjoyable experience in which I have been encouraged to think even more carefully about my relationship with you, the reader. Her illustrations have magically captured what I left lying between the lines, and they speak for themselves. Thank you, Carrie.

Not many begin writing a book, and even fewer actually finish one. With me every step of the way has been my astonishing wife, Sonia. Without her support, and especially her wonderful capacity to both surprise and delight, this book may have been finished in less time. *Grazie amore!*

Disclaimer

This is not a work of fiction. Encounters portrayed in the various vignettes, case studies and so on happened and more than once. However, to protect the identities of those involved, I have re-contextualised, amalgamated, blended, and anonymised people, events, and situations to ensure that they cannot be identified. If you imagine you see yourself or others here, it is just a coincidence, and reflects how commonplace such happenings are. The more extreme examples of emotional vandalism I have witnessed throughout 20 years working as a counsellor in and around the public, private, and third sectors have been processed through my own supervision, locked in metaphorical concrete, and dropped into the deepest ocean.

Introduction

A clinical professional decompressing after another long, emotionally draining shift scrolls down the A–Z list of courses on the website of a local university. Years of dedication, compassion, frustration, and emotional wear and tear had come to this; dreaming of another life out of scrubs. Cora found me near the bottom of the list – no offence, she added jokingly later – under "W" for *Workplace Wellbeing*. She showed her boss, who made contact on behalf of the team. Not for the first time, I explained how being overwhelmed by demand, I was taking a break from running the course to write the book. Nevertheless, I met with Cora and her colleagues; they talked, I listened, and I became even more convinced about this book's intended audience, methods, and message.

If you already work with others towards some common goal then this book is for you. It addresses the way you, your colleagues, your organisations' representatives (such as HR, management, and so on), and your context shape your wellbeing. Just look around you and see how others are not as happy and content as they ought to be, having been promised the wealth and freedom that goes with a market economy. We live in a time of disruption, where xenophobia and the cult of personality triumph over collectivism and cooperation. Younger people entering the workplace now are offered the new *normal* of an atomised, fragmentary working experience instead of the opportunity to join an organisation that can furnish them with the time and support to develop. This is why I believe that the most sustainable and enduring approach to the crisis of wellbeing is to introduce younger workers to a *Relational Approach*.

This book is not a claim to new knowledge. On the contrary, many of the ideas championed here are already out there in the academic literature. What I have done, however, is attempt to digest what I consider to be the most important, insightful, and up-to-date academic thinking and research related to flourishing at work, and present it in a form that is accessible to you, the non-specialist reader. I introduce alongside this the *Relational Approach*, a way of integrating the transformative humanistic skills and attitudes ordinarily used by counsellors and psychotherapists alike and transferring them from a therapeutic setting to the workplace. As Cora explained: *"I don't want to be a counsellor, and I don't want counselling, but I do want to know what can help"*. Accordingly, a *Relational Approach* is practical, unpretentious, and something you both use and live by. I have made it as concrete as I can through numerous tried and tested personal development and experiential exercises. The book is based on the premise that work *is* relationships. To deny this is to deny the earth spins around the sun, and I am aware that this notion was also thought far-fetched. To flourish at work we must, amongst other things, learn to navigate a complex and multi-layered system of relationships. I would be doing you a disservice to suggest the book is like a systematic manual. Perhaps it is my age, but life does not seem as simple as it did, which is why I see the ideas, values, and skills presented in the book more like a compass to navigate your way through uncertain and tricky terrain.

You may be reading this thinking you are in a uniquely dysfunctional organisation, with peculiarly odd colleagues, so in Chapters 1 and 2 I explain how it is much closer to the truth to see both as commonplace, and symptomatic of the way we unthinkingly organise ourselves. The workplace merely amplifies the beliefs and values of our prevailing political and economic structures. In our boldly agnostic scientific culture, we accept as infallible the belief we should continue to organise ourselves as chickens do, with our pecking orders. At work we avoid pain, or more specifically we ignore the big three evolutionarily important emotions of anger, fear, and shame. We bury them in something like Pandora's filing cabinet, where they languish indefinitely, because we suspect it would be hopeless to let them out and process them. At the heart of a *Relational Approach* that I introduce in Chapter 3 is the fundamental belief that hope lies in accepting we are, indeed, hopelessly and gloriously human.

The reward system in organisations relies on us gaining the trust and approval of powerful figures who have a superficial understanding of you, seeing your attempts to flourish through different eyes. In Chapter 4, I explain in detail how such narrow evaluations of what it is to be of value undermines trust in each other, triggering disruptive behaviour more akin to the playground. I also introduce the skills of Transactional Analysis, and the way they link with the transformative Relational Approach. Following on from our focus on one-to-one working relationships, Chapter 5 describes a range of democratic and ethical working practices that any organisation serious about the wellbeing of its employees must promote.

From this point onwards, the book assumes a more holistic perspective. In Chapter 6, I examine why when we come together in groups to complete tasks or share ideas, we become seduced into patterns of behaviour that disrupt what we try to do. Counsellors like myself spend a lot of time in groups defending themselves from what makes us frightened, angry, and ashamed, and it is in Chapter 7 that we make the clearest links to the fundamental motivators

Figure 0.1 Pandora's Filing Cabinet.

of emotional vandalism at work. Finally, in Chapter 8 I consider the existential arc of our working lives, and discuss the other things we do not talk about at work, including death, trauma, pain, and grief, concluding with: "so what do we do next?"

I am ambitious about what I seek to achieve here. I want more for you than to simply survive work, as if it were an unhealthy relationship where you deserve no better. Cora understood how it *was* possible to be ourselves and do something that gives our lives meaning. So, a word of caution. You may not like them, but you do have choices about your Wellbeing, and they are all Relational.

Chapter 1

Do you flourish at work?

Wellbeing – more than the absence of distress

Well … do you flourish at work? Or are you as puzzled and disconcerted by the question as I was when a well-remembered colleague took the time to ask me that question a long time ago? It troubled me then that I avoided answering truthfully by responding *yes … I am flourishing*. I instinctively understood that flourishing had to mean more than just surviving, or minimising my distress, but unfortunately that is how low many of us are prepared to set the bar when thinking about our wellbeing. So, this seems like the most obvious place to begin our conversation about what wellbeing means. A very senior manager in a large "caring" organisation explained to me how a distressed colleague had "lost their nerve", sounding oddly like how the military spoke of shell shock over a century ago. Then and now it would appear, people who experience stress at work are seen as weak, having some character flaw or lacking back-bone. Thinking of stress in this way is inappropriate and potentially dangerous. It forces the issue underground for some, and promotes a culture of shame in others that gets in the way of people either asking for help, or taking time off to get better.

Presenteeism, where people come to work even when they are feeling distressed, is ironically exacerbated both by the structure that work offers, and the normalising effect of being around colleagues who appear to be coping. At any given time, a sixth of the population goes to work experiencing the physical (somatic) symptoms of emotional distress – sleep problems, not eating properly, headaches and migraines, neck and back pains, tiredness, and more. How often do you hear people say in response to the question, "how are you doing? Oh … surviving". Sickness-presenteeism has become the "new normal" in many organisations. Researchers who want to explore the relationship between wellbeing, sickness absence, and presenteeism report how frustrating it is to persuade organisations to participate in studies because they fear "opening Pandora's box" (Collins *et al.*, 2018).

Distress is a normal reaction to abnormal circumstances. Organisations content to promote "Mental Health Awareness" seem all too blind to the ways they may contribute to creating the *abnormal circumstances* that negatively affect their employees, and instead assume that stress is inevitable, good for you, and only affects those lacking in resilience. None of this is true: every vase ultimately overflows when too much water is poured into it. We can only guess at the true scale of the distress caused by relational abuse in the workplace, because when things go wrong, workers find themselves gagged by increasingly popular non-disclosure agreements (NDAs) which protect the reputation of serial perpetrators. So-called gagging orders are becoming progressively popular in public institutions, and in the UK for instance they are used to prevent workplace abuses becoming public. The UK House of Commons, employing a mere 2,500 people, spent £2.4 million of taxpayers' money on such arrangements during 2013–17. At the time of writing, UK universities weighed in with a staggering £87 million in such pay-offs in the past two years alone, indicating how they are becoming standard practice for quietening those who they fear may harm their valuable reputations.

Soothed disengagement is not the answer. It is taken for granted that wellbeing is in the control of the worker, and that stress equates to some personal irresponsibility in how you run your life. Affordable spa weekends, yoga courses, worthy yet vacuous slogans, and dry Januarys are just some aspects of the burgeoning industry of stress management and wellbeing products that place the responsibility for being well firmly with *you*. Nobody argues that having a band play as the ship sinks can help soothe, but doing so is a potentially fatal distraction from the business of avoiding icebergs to begin with. As a hospital doctor explained: "It is put on me as an individual to adapt and survive this environment ... rather than making the environment more survivable ... sitting in a room trying not to think about stuff is not the answer". When talking about resilience training she went on to explain: "if someone is beating you with a stick do you offer them padding (i.e. more training) so they can carry on hitting you?" It does not take much imagination to recognise that colleagues too overworked to attend their subsidised mindfulness course or complete their online wellbeing module will soon become resentful about being offered psychological personal protective equipment (PPE) to guard against the emotional risks of their workplace. Organisations recognise the problem at some level, regularly offering expensive interventions such as one-to-one coaching to employees of strategic importance. Yet it is an act of faith to assume that the feel-good factor of wellbeing will "trickle-down" the organisation. The danger of the beer and circuses approach is that we become seduced into pathologising the individual, ignoring the underlying structural causes of distress, and passively accepting palliative care as the solution.

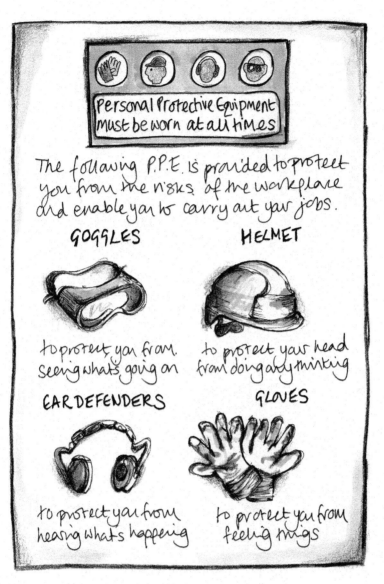

Personal Protective Equipment must be worn at all times

The following P.P.E. is provided to protect you from the risks of the workplace and enable you to carry out your jobs.

GOGGLES

HELMET

to protect you from seeing what's going on

to protect your head from doing any thinking

EAR DEFENDERS

GLOVES

to protect you from hearing what's happening

to protect you from feeling things

Figure 1.1 PPE – Protection from thinking, feeling, hearing or seeing.

A multi-layered phenomenon. I do not accept that the absence of stress is sufficient to render the workplace somewhere we can thrive as human beings. In order to flourish we must consider how the individual and the organisation or groups of people interact and engage with each other. Organisations are not wholly responsible for the stress we experience at work. It is too simplistic to attach blame to either the individual or a faceless monolith. Instead, stress has to be understood in terms of a multi-layered physiological, social and political phenomenon. A *Relational Approach*, which I champion here, emphasises connectedness, complexity, and mutuality. It considers the holistic wellbeing of an individual and how this is entangled with the wellbeing of the community to which he or she belongs. Organisational and structural factors frustrate and impede healthy ways of organising our working lives (Chapters 2 and 8). Our default relational (Chapters 3–5) and group behaviours (Chapter 6) also contribute to a potent shadow-side of work which manifests itself in emergent behaviours, which includes relational abuse (Chapter 7). You may be disappointed to learn that I am not offering any psychological quick fixes to survive what can feel like an abusive relationship with your place of work. The more ambitious project for us all is to understand, and then renegotiate aspects of how we see ourselves in relationship with our work communities, because such relationships can inadvertently undermine our capacity to flourish.

Neoliberalism and the wellbeing agenda. Forty years ago we seemed to stop trusting governments to organise our social structures and make sense of the world for us. Instead, we put our faith in the free market, where the average of the expressed preferences of countless consumers becomes the process through which we resolve our social problems. There are drastic consequences for our wellbeing as the state withdraws from health care, energy supply, housing, law and order, telecommunications, and public transport. Instead of a share in the prosperity, we get impending climate catastrophe, populist convulsions, public health emergencies and banking crises. We thought we were getting freedom, but instead neoliberalism offers us inequality and envy to spur us on to work harder, be more productive, and so increase our value in the marketplace. The CEO in a FTSE 100 company now earns about of 150 times the average salary compared to only 50 times that amount in 1998. Income inequality – which affects levels of trust, social interaction, mental illness, hostility, violence, racism, and what the Institute for Fiscal Studies calls "deaths of despair" (i.e. early deaths from alcohol/drug abuse and suicide linked to poverty and social isolation) – have become the characteristics of our hitherto cooperative species (Beattie, 2019).

The neoliberal era has seen an erosion of the power of unions and employee collectives to influence working conditions, with the management caste in our organisations resembling "oligarchies" or private dictatorships. The current generation of young people are increasingly aware of their expendability. The shifting dependence of our universities towards external funding has meant that they too have fallen to market forces and an obsession with rankings (Chapter 2). Universities have lost their role as a place of learning, becoming instead cathedrals of bureaucracy (Bal, 2017). The consequences are dire because academics and researchers who would otherwise challenge the structural problems of the workplace have surrendered to the same managerialism sweeping through other professions.

Control of the "wellbeing agenda" is less about compassion and empathy and more about market share and political kudos. A key driver for contemporary organisations is how wellbeing relates to productivity and ultimately profit. We all recognise the benefits to an organisation of reduced sickness absence, staff turnover, and attrition through workplace conflicts to its clients, patients, trading partners, students, customers, etc. Yet how interested are organisations in accepting responsibility for their role in workplace discord? It will take time to challenge the myth that the atomised workplace frees us from the weakness and shame of interdependence, because the opposite is true. Having the solid support of a collective is the definition of strength. The greatest difficulty we face, which we examine in Chapter 3, is the anxiety we feel about learning to tolerate those who we rely on for our survival. Will it require a global public health calamity to act as unwelcome midwife to once radical ideas about how we organise ourselves?

Safety was the low-lying fruit; the more ambitious project promotes our *Health*

The management standards approach. There continue to be physical hazards in the workplace, but in neoliberal *service-based* economies such as the US and UK, risk increasingly relates to the way that work is organised; harm is more likely to be emotional than physical. Framed as it is in risk management, in 2004 the UK Health and Safety Executive (HSE) produced standards that address the six primary – and overlapping – sources of stress (or distress) at work:

- *Role*: Whether people are clear about their role, and its expectations within the organisation (see *Psychological Contract* – Chapter 2).
- *Relationships*: The quality of our relationship with others is the most important factor contributing to our overall wellbeing (Chapters 3 and 4). Conflict is the most frequently reported source of problems and distress in many occupations. It may also be indicative of more serious workplace problems including emotional abuse (Chapter 7).
- *Control*: Jobs with high demands or time pressure but low levels of empowerment are "high-strain" and bear the greatest risk of emotional harm (Henderson *et al.*, 2013). Autonomy over workload encompasses the invidious issue of micromanagement (Chapter 4).

- *Support*: Work is about a search for daily meaning as well as daily bread, for recognition as well as cash. Support includes showing encouragement, appreciation, and offering sponsorship, which in concrete form means being given the resources to do your job. Hearing you are valued in your work is a vital source of pride and dignity (Chapter 5).
- *Demands*: This asks organisations to take seriously the physical, emotional, and cognitive demands on employees. Working hard can be stimulating, and good facilities convey that employees are valued. Yet who gets to define working *too hard* and *good* facilities (Chapter 6)?
- *Change*: This relates to how change in organisations, be it large or small, is understood, managed, and communicated (Chapter 8). Too much change or mismanaged changed is stressful, and leaves a memory in the organisation. Long-term follow-up of companies who have gone through downsizing shows that even amongst the employees who did not lose their jobs, rates of mental illness and sickness absence remained high for up to 10 years (Bhui *et al.*, 2012).

The management standards are undoubtedly helpful for raising awareness of stress in the workplace, and providing busy administrators with a framework to navigate the relational, cultural, political, and organisational complexities of stress. However, when seen through the lens of risk management, efforts to address stress become superficial. Actions are reduced to technical fixes for harm prevention rather than an opportunity to consider the structural solutions for promoting health. Perhaps understandably, the levels of risk identified amongst the mountains of Stress Risk Assessments across the country rarely moves above Low–Medium, because managers mark their own homework. High risk would indicate a crisis, and that is more difficult to ignore.

The HSE management standards are also useful for structuring staff surveys and, in principle, benchmarking both internally and nationally. This perhaps explains why organisations feel reluctant about using them, preferring instead to craft meaningless questionnaires that seek to congratulate management on their efforts. For medium to large organisations, HSE standards can lead to such an unmanageable volume of data that managers, H&S, and HR professionals feel like they are drinking water from a fire hose. The timing of staff surveys is also problematic and open to manipulation. For organisations subject to seasonal variations of workload and workflow, and for those undergoing perennial re-structuring and internal change, there is never a good time to ask, "how are you feeling?" In any case, as the saying goes, the dogs bark, and the caravan moves on.

Crucially, the HSE management standards acknowledge that at the heart of every risk to our wellbeing lies a deficit in the so-called soft skills or relational competencies. It is this deficit in relational competencies that I seek to address here through the exploration and promotion of a *Relational Approach*.

Other indicators of distress. Given that stress is subject to cultural, class, and gendered biases, it is instructive to consider links to other, perhaps more subtle indicators of whether people are thriving in the workplace.

Employee assistance programmes (EAPs), which evolved to manage alcohol abuse in the USA, were designed to assist organisations manage issues affecting worker productivity. Studies examining the link between rates of EAP use and wellbeing suggest that their usefulness and return on investment for the organisation are largely a matter of faith (Joseph *et al.*, 2018).

Churn. Recruitment and retention can, depending on its scale, be costly in terms of advertising, screening, interviewing, appointment, induction, and training. Whilst low levels of "churn" are healthy for an organisation, spikes can indicate localised problems. For teaching and nursing where stress is endemic, high turnover and retention are synonymous with the professions. HR professionals consider exit interviews unreliable, only offering disgruntled exiteers an opportunity to grind their axes, preferring instead to gag them with cash incentives. Yet in my personal experience such people can have a genuine desire to provide supportive and constructive feedback to prevent repeats of their own sometimes painful experiences.

Trade unions are shown to improve workplace wellbeing through a civilising process that mediates organisational change, improves pay, and working conditions etc. (Bryson *et al.*, 2013). Individuals, teams, or groups that generate unusually large amounts of casework for a trade union may indicate the presence of deeper issues undermining employee wellbeing. However, the absence of busy caseloads may not necessarily mean that all is well. In the UK, workers are not compelled to join trade unions, which means that in principle employees can have a "free-ride" and gain all the benefits of a unionised workplace without actually belonging to one. Given this, one might expect to see a reasonably random distribution of wellbeing across an organisation irrespective of whether someone belongs to a union. Surprisingly, however, studies show that higher levels of job satisfaction and wellbeing are observed amongst unionised workers than non-members (Haile *et al.*, 2015). Given that more than a third of non-members belonged to the managerial and supervisory ranks in this study, it is not surprising that unionisation, which is likely to limit their customary authority, adversely affects job satisfaction, health, and wellbeing.

The science of wellbeing

The medical model and distress. We are all impressed by the success of empirical science, and medicine in particular. A clearly defined disease or pathology, such as Type 1 diabetes, can be understood at the molecular level and is treated with life-transforming success. The so-called medical model of cause and effect seduces us into positivist ways of understanding human distress and despair that are, I believe, unhelpful. It invites judgements about illness, health, what is normal, and more worryingly, what is abnormal. In seeking a medical basis for distress, we distract ourselves from examining the underlying psychosocial shapers of what and how we feel. Practitioners, researchers, and scholars alike have trouble agreeing where the dividing line between psychological wellbeing and disturbance lies. Perhaps it is because there is none? Psychological health is a continuum, and we all move along it from time to time, some more than others, but it is a continuum nevertheless.

Wellbeing and the workplace. Unlike the natural sciences with its universally accepted understanding of key dimensions (i.e. mass, time, length, etc.), researchers and scholars in the humanities struggle to reach a consensus on what it means to be well and healthy. This explains why related terms such as mental health, resilience, and wellbeing remain somewhat vague and difficult to define. The debate about their meaning will go on for some time because of the political and ideological nature of such terms. Well-meaning neoliberals add to the confusion by introducing all manner of new and spurious terms, unwittingly revealing their own ideological stance about how *worth* equates to some notion of what it is to be *normal*. Adding to the confusion, the powerful voice of the World Health Organisation further conflates terms like stress, normal, mental health, and wellbeing:

> A state of wellbeing in which every individual realises his or her own potential, can cope with the normal stresses of life, can work productively and fruitfully and is able to make a contribution to her or his community.

Early attempts to define wellbeing were framed in terms of a deficit of pathology, or the *absence* of mental illness, so measurement scales were shaped by the constructs of anxiety and depression. Trying to measure and quantify wellbeing along the dimensions of pleasure (hedonism) and virtue (eudemonism) is fraught with difficulty, because such concepts overlap in ways that are hard or even impossible to untangle. What gets lost when we try to dissect the lived experience of a holistic person is precisely the complexity of what emerges through our inter-relatedness (Chapter 6). Furthermore, thinking of wellbeing as an absence of the kind of stress described by the HSE management standards blinds us to the incompatibility of the two concepts. Consider for a moment how *optimism*, which arguably contributes to our holistic sense of wellbeing, can potentially undermine our health (see Box 1.1). The overly optimistic mountaineer taking chances with their equipment and weather engages in the kind of risky behaviour that can lead to calamity.

Attempting to draw a line around a person at work, separating them from their life beyond, is also as artificial as it seems (Figure 1.2). This is especially

Figure 1.2 Attempting to draw a line around a person.

so for those of us who see the workplace as our major source of social and personal esteem, or even amorous interest. Does the workplace end when you put your smartphone on silent, snap your laptop closed, clock-out at the end of the day, or take your uniform off? More worryingly, does work only end when you finish your second bottle of wine or sink your fourth pint on a Wednesday evening? Artificial boundaries around our work and non-work identities reflect an impoverished notion of what it means to be a human being. The holistic, context-free perspective of wellbeing cannot possibly disentangle an individual's general wellbeing from other parts of their *lifeworld* (*lebenswelt*) as the philosopher Jürgen Habermas calls it, which includes time spent at work. Although inequality and instrumentality are exacerbated, and even amplified by the structures of the workplace, the injuries to our wellbeing merely reflect what goes on in the wider world.

Box 1.1 The elements of wellbeing

A check-list based on the key elements shown below form the basis of the wellbeing inventory in Longo *et al.* (2018). Take a moment to reflect on how you are feeling today, and complete the questionnaire (Exercise 1.1). Return to it in a couple of weeks and see if the outcome has changed. Can you identify where these changes have occurred; in work or beyond?

- *Awareness* – knowing yourself, and being in touch with how you feel.
- *Calmness* – feeling serene and peaceful.
- *Competence* – able to overcome challenges and achieve outcomes.
- *Congruence* – the perception that what you do is compatible with your interests, values, and beliefs.
- *Connection* – having relationships that are supportive and rewarding.
- *Development* – a commitment to improving, developing, and advancing.
- *Happy* – a cheerful and satisfied demeanour.
- *Involved* – engaged and interested in what you do, and who you do it with.
- *Optimism* – having a positive outlook on, and expectations about, the future.
- *Purpose* – a sense of direction and meaning in your life.
- *Self-acceptance* – living with the way you are, including any ambiguity.
- *Self-worth* – liking yourself, but recognising the line where narcissism begins.
- *Significance* – believing what we do is worthwhile, rewarding, and valuable.
- *Vital* – energetic and full of life.

Exercise 1.1 The 14-item scales of general wellbeing

Instructions. Below you will find 14 statements about your experiences. Indicate how true each statement is regarding the experiences in your life overall. There are no right or wrong answers. Please choose the answer that best reflects your experience rather than what you think your experience should be.

	Not at all true	A bit true	Somewhat true	Mostly true	Very true
1. I feel happy	☐	☐	☐	☐	☐
2. I feel energetic	☐	☐	☐	☐	☐
3. I feel calm	☐	☐	☐	☐	☐
4. I'm optimistic	☐	☐	☐	☐	☐
5. In my activities, I feel absorbed by what I'm doing	☐	☐	☐	☐	☐
6. I'm in touch with how I really feel inside	☐	☐	☐	☐	☐
7. I accept most aspects of myself	☐	☐	☐	☐	☐
8. I feel great about myself	☐	☐	☐	☐	☐
9. I am highly effective at what I do	☐	☐	☐	☐	☐
10. I feel I am improving	☐	☐	☐	☐	☐
11. I have a purpose	☐	☐	☐	☐	☐
12. What I do in my life is worthwhile	☐	☐	☐	☐	☐
13. What I do is consistent with what I believe I should do	☐	☐	☐	☐	☐
14. I feel close and connected to the people around me	☐	☐	☐	☐	☐

© Longo, Coyne & Joseph.

The humanistic workplace

Psychotherapy has been preoccupied with pathology, despair, and anguish for much of the twentieth century. However, a growing body of scholars and practitioners are turning their attention to how we actively flourish and prosper as human beings. Humanists such as Carl Rogers, Eric Erikson and Jürgen Habermas – who we will hear more from later – and positive psychologists such as Martin Seligman (2000) are interested, as am I, in the personal, relational and systemic aspects of what it means to flourish and thrive. The focus is on our capacity to nurture and be nurtured, have the personal courage to be our real selves, develop our interpersonal skills, and foster the capacity to trust in the workplace. This is a far more ambitious project than simply avoiding what harms us. Wellbeing then is about *your* subjective perception of being happy, and means promoting *your* sense of purpose in the workplace.

Authenticity, congruence, and the good life. Thinking about the good life is marked in terms of millennia. Modern philosophers believe that the pursuit of *both* pleasure (hedonism) and virtue (eudemonism) produce the greatest overall wellbeing. The former is to do with "hot-brain" processing and focuses on fast, subjective judgements about what feels pleasant in the "here and now". The latter describes "cold-brain" processing, or longer-term evaluations of one's life. It is about doing things we consider worthy and consistent with our values and self-identity. For Sigmund Freud (1856–1939), it was simple: "we want to become happy, and then remain so". When asked what a healthy person should be able to do well, his response was equally unfussy: "Lieben und arbeiten", or *to love and to work*. He felt it was such a waste to settle for superficial happiness (hedonism), or as the HSE would suggest, set ourselves the unambitious target of avoiding unhappiness, achieved by either avoiding human relationships (see Chapter 3), or soothed disengagement, i.e. numbing with alcohol, drugs, food, social media, watching sport, or working too hard. *We thrive when the physical, intellectual, emotional, relational, and spiritual domains of what it is to be human are given the opportunity to be expressed.*

A person living authentically can accurately match his or her own experience to their awareness, and is congruent in their self-expression, living life with little fear of what other people think about them. The humanistic notion of congruence is more than being just honest with someone, however. It needs to be concerned with a relationship dynamic rather than your own personal view of the world. Compare, "to be *honest* Theresa, you are a real nightmare to work with", with "working together feels difficult for me … how about you Theresa?" The former is judgemental and blaming, while the latter demonstrates that we have reflected on what we might bring to our relationships. Carl Rogers promoted the simple (although devilishly difficult in practice) idea that interpersonal relationships characterised by congruence, empathy and acceptance are sufficient not just for the *good life*, but for profound therapeutic change for those experiencing distress (Rogers, 1967). Offering this type of relationship is not so much about *doing*, but *being*. The person-centred counsellor or psychotherapist will tell you that learning to do this takes practice and lifelong reflectivity.

Inauthenticity – the art of putting on a show. Traditionally, workers were paid only to do physical things with their bodies, such as lifting, digging, and so on. However, increasingly in Western service-based economies, the performance of technical tasks requires a mixture of thinking *and* relational skills. What is not so obvious about this relatively new arrangement of exchange – which we explore in more detail in Chapter 2 – is that now we have to manage how and what we *feel* when we work. You might reflect on how true this may be of your own work setting. Professions that most readily come to mind include policing, prison work, health care, social work, teaching, hospitality, human resources, etc. The physician, midwife, or nurse who invest time and energy to empathise with and reassure apprehensive patients on a daily basis are to be congratulated for their "bedside manner". A personable tiller at an increasingly rare checkout can make a trip to the supermarket a highlight for the socially isolated in our communities. In these and other roles, our skill in managing and projecting our emotions can be sold for a wage, and as such they have a kind of exchange value, albeit one that is taken for granted. It is a depressing reflection of our neoliberal economies, where it is possible to make money without adding value in any real way to things, that the exchange value of our emotional labour is quite so low. Compare the incomes of those who volunteer their time to care for the most vulnerable in our society (i.e. pre-school children, the unwell, and elderly), and the suburban gauchos found herding noisy packs of other people's pets through our public spaces.

The sociologist Arlie Hochschild (1983) recognised that the settings in which we work invite us to separate how we feel on the inside with how we appear on the outside, in much the same way an actor does. We do it through either deep *method* acting, where we try really hard to recreate the feelings that must be expressed, *or* through *surface* acting, where we put on the expected mask by faking or supressing emotions. When Stanislavski developed his famous training method for actors, he explained: "all action must have an inner justification, be logical, coherent and real". Or as Marlon Brando put it: "to be believable … it has to hurt a little". When we are being our *authentic selves*, our emotions are spontaneously and genuinely experienced. Here, there is neither need nor time to act, only to *be* what Carl Rogers termed congruent. Doing emotional labour is linked to our emotional intelligence, which describes our capacity to perceive others accurately and to understand, appraise, and express our own emotions. Having to *do* emotional labour is not in itself harmful to our wellbeing, but the tension of chronic inauthenticity, which means regularly engaging in surface acting to supress our authentic selves, consistently predicts job dis-satisfaction, withdrawal from work, staff turnover, stress, and ultimately burnout (Figure 1.3). Mounting our own personal campaign of working to rule, like the jobsworth who conforms to the letter of their role, can minimise exposure to emotional work through avoidance (Chapter 3).

Staying emotionally safe at work. Doing "surface acting" or being incongruent is not always motivated by cynicism. Surviving the emotional attrition and everyday traumas in some professions requires an emotional shutting-down simply to survive, in the short term at least (Chapter 8). People who seek

Figure 1.3 The Emotional Labourer.

to avoid emotional engagement and shield who they are may be drawn to a particular profession where authenticity is a distinct disadvantage, i.e. working as a prison officer, where any vulnerability can be mercilessly exploited. Living in our heads is an effective strategy to avoid the messy business of human relationships. Having worked in universities and healthcare settings for over 30 years, I see how an environment that prizes the world of the mind offers many hiding places for our vulnerabilities. Acknowledging vulnerability or authenticity at work is risky because it invites stigma or being seen as weak, inadequate or dispensable. Consider our sexual orientation, which can be invisible compared to any of our other social identities. Lesbian, gay, bisexual, trans, and queer (LGBTQ) employees must make a conscious cost–benefit analysis when weighing up whether to come out at work, i.e. the threat of stigma versus being openly authentic (Baker & Lucas, 2017). Strategies used to minimise the risk of authenticity in such circumstances include seeking safe spaces, which means finding employment in industries, communities, cities, and geographic regions with a reputation for being more liberal and accepting of difference.

For the time being at least, authenticity and congruence in the workplace come at a price, because we cannot always trust to be met as a person there. So until things change, and they will eventually, I want the ideas and values of this book to accompany you until change does happen and you can put them into practice. People instinctively know what they need to flourish, and a *Relational Approach* facilitates that process.

Things to keep in mind

- We most readily think of wellbeing as the absence of stress, which can be achieved through a mixture of soothed disengagement and avoidance, but avoiding stress is just an aspect of what it means to flourish at work.
- It will take time to challenge the myth that the atomised workplace frees us from the weakness and shame of interdependence when the opposite is in fact true. Individual wellbeing is intimately enmeshed with the wellbeing of the communities to which we belong.
- A *Relational Approach* is grounded in the humanistic tradition, which prizes congruence, empathy, and acceptance of self *and* others.
- Trust is the key. Authenticity will remain a risky business until we can learn to trust and be met with compassion as a person at work.

References

Baker SJ & Lucas K. (2017). Is it safe to bring myself to work? Understanding LGBTQ experiences of workplace dignity. *Canadian Journal of Administrative Sciences*, 34, 133–148.

Bal M. (2017). *Dignity in the workplace: New theoretical perspectives*. Basingstoke: Palgrave Macmillan.

Beattie P. (2019). The road to psychopathology. Neoliberalism and the human mind. *Journal of Social Issues*, 75(1), 89–112.

Bhui KS, Dinos S, Stansfeld SA, & White PD. (2012). A synthesis of the evidence for managing stress at work: A review of the reviews reporting on anxiety, depression, and absenteeism. *Journal of Environmental and Public Health*, 2012, Article ID 515874, doi:10.1155/2012/515874.

Bryson A, Barth E, & Dale-Olsen H. (2013). The effects of organizational change on worker well-being and the moderating role of trade unions. *Industrial and Labor Review*, 66(4), 989–1011.

Collins AM, Cartwright S, & Cowlishaw S. (2018). Sickness presenteeism and sickness absence over time: A UK employee perspective. *Work & Stress. An International Journal of Work, Health & Organisations*, 32(1), 68–83.

Haile G, Bryson A, & White M. (2015). Spillover effects of unionisation on non-members' wellbeing. *Labour Economics*, 35, 108–122.

Henderson C, Williams P, Little K, & Thornicroft G. (2013). Mental health problems in the workplace: Changes in employers' knowledge, attitudes and practices in England 2006–2010. *The British Journal of Psychiatry*, 202, s70–76.

Hochschild AR (1983). *The managed heart: Commercialization of human feeling*. Berkeley: University of California Press.

Joseph B, Walker A, & Fuller-Tyszkiewicz M. (2018). Evaluating the effectiveness of employee assistance programmes: a systematic review. *European Journal of Work and Organizational Psychology*, 27(1), 1–15.

Longo Y, Coyne I, & Joseph S. (2018). Development of the short version of the scales of general well-being: The 14 item SGWB. *Personality and Individual Differences*, 124, 31–34.

Rogers CR. (1967). *On becoming a person: A therapist's view of psychotherapy*. London: Constable.

Seligman MEP & Csikszentmihalyi M. (2000). Positive psychology: An introduction. *American Psychologist*, 55, 5–14.

Chapter 2

Our invisible cage

The illusion of choice

The eyes see only what the mind is prepared to comprehend. The story goes that when asked by an avid devotee "who are you?", the Buddha replied, "*I am awake*"! This does not mean the Buddha suffered from insomnia, but that he was alert to the dangers of being "*entangled in the tangle*", or possessing a narrow attentional spotlight as opposed to seeing the bigger picture. There is a lot of talk currently about unconscious bias and woke culture, which are ideas or movements that seek to draw attention to those things, often out of awareness that influence how we live and the decisions we make. Our *lifeworld* stands behind each of us who participate in life, and is ordinarily so unproblematic that we are incapable of making ourselves aware of it. In terms of biases, our memory, for example, cannot truly be relied on because it tends to order events not by time but by their importance to us, which changes across our lifespan. Relying on experience is also a risky strategy. It often takes someone from *outside* a given discipline to facilitate a leap forwards because such people are unconstrained by the "common sense" or dogmatic notions associated with a given profession. Organisations that consider themselves bastions of certainty in an uncertain world prize confident projections about the future over the reality of uncertainty and ambiguity. Delusions of infallibility and narcissism at the top of our organisations leads to tokenism around consultation with its members. *Hypernormalisation* is as much a part of modern life as it was in the time of the Buddha. We create a more acceptable version of reality because we cannot tolerate the precarious foundations of our social world. People accept as normal those situations that they know are not right, either because they think there is no alternative, or because of a cynical denial of personal responsibility (Bal, 2017).

Our *lifeworld* includes the culture into which we are born; it confers on us all kinds of subtle and not-so-subtle conditions, rules, expectations, and demands. It is easy to accept these rules unquestioningly as the only way to arrange our lives. Powerful influencers such as religions, political parties, the media, the social class to which we belong or aspire to, and of course friends, teachers, peers, and colleagues, envelop us, shape our beliefs, and our attitudes to life. As we grow and develop we accept as obvious and unchallengeable evaluations (often called introjects) taken in from such external sources. My white, Eurocentric worldview became painfully apparent on my first trip to east Africa, where it was pointed out that a zebra is in fact a black animal with white stripes, and not the other way around. We inherit our worldview through systems of thinking and perceiving, typically unaware that our relationships are shaped and limited by hypernormal assumptions that act like the bars of some invisible cage. It need not be this way. Increasing our awareness of the background consensus in our everyday lives, and the structural inequalities embedded in how we organise ourselves is the first step towards changing things for the better.

False consciousness and the Iron Law. Much of what is hypernormal about contemporary working life began to emerge towards the end of the nineteenth century. In seeking to understand our social evolution, Karl Marx and Frederick Engels pessimistically suggested that it was not the consciousness of people that determines our being but, on the contrary, our social being that determines our consciousness. We are seduced, they argued, by legal, economic, bureaucratic, and political superstructures into a false consciousness that sees us toiling towards goals that are not necessarily in our interest (Marx & Engels, 1977). The arbitrary power relations in our society continue to hold sway over us precisely because "they have not been seen through". The old conundrum of whether our agency as individuals can resist the alienating repression of the systems in which we live has exercised humanists for decades (Chapter 3). "Matter or mind, *no matter*, mind or matter, *never mind*" captures the essence of the worn-out dilemma of living between necessity and freedom (Merquior, 1986).

Robert Michels (1876–1936) introduced his somewhat pessimistic *Iron Law* a little later describing how, despite our best intentions, all worker democracies ultimately degenerate into oligarchic bureaucracies dominated by a closed managerial caste. Although this does indeed happen a lot, it is also a form of false consciousness because it is not inevitable, and it need not be this way (Diefenbach, 2019). The so-called *Iron Law* introduces numerous unsavoury and familiar hypernormal assumptions about how we organise the workplace, including the necessity for workers to undergo comprehensive specialisation and separation of tasks. This prepares the way for the creation of an expert leadership class who are thought – as a matter of faith – to possess skills and abilities impossible to find in the rank-and-file. Ideas such as job rotation, particularly for tasks requiring specialist "leadership expertise", makes no sense at all if you believe that management is a specialism. Yet this is how power becomes concentrated amongst organisational elites, paving the way for a male-dominated management professional caste (more about gender later).

This manager caste, begotten and not made remember, can only exist if there is some social stratification, or a separation of the workforce into two groups – the great apathetic, compliant, untalented masses, and a few socially dominant peacocks. It appears self-evidently the best way to organise ourselves. Indeed, dominant hierarchies are quite common in the natural world for organising birds (especially chickens with their *pecking order*), baboons, and wolves; but in the case of contemporary human beings it is a model applied to the wrong species.

Hypernormalisation appears to be a useful tactic to help us survive and take part in society, but it also limits our potential and forces us to conform to an impoverished notion of what it is to be human. In swallowing-whole ideas that seem to be obvious and apparently true, we unwittingly undermine our own capacity to live well. It was in despair that the sociologist Max Weber (1864–1920) coined the term *Iron Cage* to describe what he saw as the inexorable disappearance of our will and autonomy to the blind career of the machine (Figure 2.1). The highly influential and, I feel, more optimistic philosopher Jürgen Habermas sees our modern condition as a kind of painful tug-of-war between our *lifeworld* and the unyielding, alienating elements of our capitalist system, conditioned by money and market power, both of which are tied to bureaucracy and hierarchy (Pusey, 1987). But the bars of the cage are gossamer thin and arbitrary, like cobwebs, not rigid and inflexible at all. If we understand the truth of this, then things can change. If we brush away the cobwebs, we can see ourselves and others more clearly, broaden our appreciation of our emotional world and, more importantly, see how others might see their world too. So, I want to examine in more detail some of the assumptions that shape our workplace, and challenge their hypernormality in contemporary organisations. Does this false consciousness work for you? Does it undermine your attempts to flourish? Which side of the relational seam that knits together our lifeworld and systems must shift for us to achieve a more harmonious life?

The scientific management of relationships

The atomised workplace. For nearly four decades, neoliberalist ideology has shaped our global economy. With the authority and inescapability of scientific laws, we have sacrificed our social interests on the high altar of investor confidence. It has become hypernormal for all things to benefit from the market, where invisible, amoral forces weed out the weak and prioritise according to growth, productivity, and efficiency. State-led economies have fallen from favour, only to be replaced by outsourcing, floods of foreign capital, privatisation, and food banks for the unlucky. The idea of governments being responsible for welfare has given way to expectations of individual responsibility and competitiveness. We have relinquished protection from our employers, distributive

Figure 2.1 Holy Shit!

equality, access to essential services, and environmental sustainability for the cult of individualism. This is having disastrous consequences for our wellbeing. *Scientific Management*, pioneered by Fred Taylor at the dawn of the last century (1911), has received a new lease of life for managing an atomised, untrustworthy workforce who can be reduced to "cogs" in an organisational machine. Concerns about the dehumanising effects of *Scientific Management* led to the development of worker communities such as Bourneville and Port Sunlight in the UK, where the focus was on people as a resource, to be "socialised and Christianised" for the good of business relations. Such a *Human Resource* (HR) approach was not so much a departure from *Scientific Management*, but an extension of it. Both seek to exert control over workers by either manipulating or avoiding relationships, but the HR philosophy is especially seductive. It breaches the boundaries between our work and non-work selves, and prizes worker autonomy only if it aligns with what the machine wants. You can manage your own time flexibly so long as you submit to surveillance (see *The Panopticon* – Chapter 7).

Order, control, sex, and gender. For trail-blazing civil rights activists such as Ruth Ginsburg it made perfect sense at one time to use the terms sex and gender interchangeably, because the former "meant only one thing" to the overwhelmingly male population of US lawmakers in the past. Yet during pregnancy, my wife was regularly and confusingly asked, even by health professionals, *what gender are you having?*, reflecting our ongoing hypernormal assumptions about sex, gender, and control. Sex in this context describes our biological differences, i.e. male and female, while gender refers to the complex social practices used to build our identity from the expectations, attitudes, behaviours, values, stereotypes, and ideologies that permeate the culture associated with our sex (Fine, 2017). Gender is about what we do – it describes our *behaviour*. It is how we learn to "do this" under some circumstances, and "not to do that", under others. Men of my age will understand how satnav technology rescues us from asking directions when lost. We need no longer wind down the car window and risk our membership of the "real man club" by admitting we are not competent and in control.

Expectant parents have been able to determine the sex of their unborn children since the 1970s when obstetric ultrasound first began to enter the mainstream. This medically useless information only cements our expectations of gender, and undermines Jean-Jacques Rousseau's optimism in his *Social Contract* from over two hundred years ago that claimed we were *born free*. The blue paint in the metaphorical nurseries of every little boy, symbolising their un-earnt male privilege, is long dry before he even puts in an appearance. The political power of gender is a deadly serious matter. An estimated 126 million females who *should* have come into existence up until 2010 have not done so because of selective foeticide linked to obstetric ultrasound (Grech, 2015). It has been recognised for some time that organisations are gendered; advantage and disadvantage, exploitation and control, action and emotion are organised in terms of whether you are a man or a woman. While masculine ideals of order, control, hierarchy, and domination are not *essential*, which is to say they are not qualities intrinsic to our biology, they do seem to be useful if we wish to progress in the workplace. In reality, it is more complicated than this because gender does not stand alone in shaping what informs inequality or exclusion in the workplace. Other differences intersect gender in this respect, including age, sexuality, ethnicity, disability, and of course social class (Acker, 2012). A white middle-class man worries less about feeling included at the office than, say, a black working-class woman.

When Joan Acker began thinking about gender bias, people in paid employment could look forward to a lifetime of service with a single employer. Relationships between workers and their bosses were relatively stable and characterised by collective representation by trade unions. Loyalty was rewarded with a pension, gradual career progression, and job security. A job description – which sets out criteria like qualifications, skill, complexity, and effort required – remains the building block of our rational bureaucracies. It has the worthy intention of replacing informal practices with more formal scientific processes that aim to meet the higher needs of the organisation over those of corruptible individuals (see Chapter 7). The rational bureaucracy adopts a transactional approach to employment, and assumes that people are fundamentally lazy and untrustworthy resources to be motivated, managed, and instrumentalised through scientific job selection.

A job is like a box, a thing apart into which a person must fit. The underlying logic is that we employ a disembodied, gender-neutral "vanilla" type of worker to fit into the box. Although the intention is fairness, the unintended consequences are far from this. Every job in an organisation is shaped by the unstated and inherently masculine preoccupation with order, control and domination: the colour of the box is decidedly *blue*. In the face of this apparently rational and fair arrangement, structural inequality becomes *hypernormal*. It is so deeply engrained that we no longer see that the experience of work is typically male, and not necessarily typically human. The very notion of a hypothetical worker excludes by definition people with bodies that reproduce, experience the menopause, become ill, are disabled by their built environment, become distressed, or who do not want to play the game of masculine domination and control.

The tension between production and reproduction. A huge body of research now supports Acker's theoretical claim that the hypernormal idea of jobs in hierarchies, so often used by managers to exert control in organisations, disadvantages women, people with other intersecting characteristics, and men who choose not to conform to a stereotype (Britton & Logan, 2008). To achieve the qualities of a hypothetical worker we need to become just like a stereotypical man whose life is centred on *production* through a full-time, life-long, all-consuming job. Meanwhile, the thoroughly exhausting and fundamental work of *reproduction*, which is about creating life and sustaining relationships (e.g. who picks up the phone at home, keeps up with friends, plans meals, etc.?), and of supporting the stereotypical man, is usually, but not always, achieved through the support of a woman (see stay-at-home fathers in Chapter 8). Industrialisation has segregated men, women, and our children in a way which does not reflect how we got here as a species. Women are signalled early in their careers that traditional male traits are expected for senior roles, and that promotion depends on their ability to act like their male counterparts; "I did not realise I had to be a man to get to the top", is a comment I have heard many times. The pressure to postpone pregnancy or even relent on the aspiration of having children are examples of just how women are invited to comply with the ideal of the hypothetical worker. In the USA, insurance companies now invite women to put their *eggs on ice* with the dubious promise of starting families later in their career. Because the abstract worker in fact corresponds to the Protestant man of vocation, then his body, minimal responsibility for child rearing, and the control of emotions pervades our work processes and contributes to our invisible cage.

The knowledge-based economy has created millions of jobs that did not exist 30 years ago. Workers now expect to change their employer frequently in search of better opportunities or in response to job insecurity that goes along with downsizing, lay-offs, and mergers. Technology facilitates the mobile *precariat* who are told that the rhythm and timing of our work (*production*) is now better adapted to our commitments outside (i.e. *reproduction*). A certain version of feminism has entered a dangerous liaison with neoliberalism, one which prizes individual achievement, responsibility for women's own welfare, and competitiveness. So-called empowerment has become overwhelmingly interpreted as "womenomics", or the segregation of more and more women into less well-paid precarious work (Eisenstein, 2017). According to the *World Economic Forum*, three-quarters of cashiers in shops are women: nearly all of them are expected to lose their jobs with increasing automation.

The gender gap in the STEM (science, technology, engineering, and mathematics) subjects means masculine biases go unchallenged in the evolving field of Artificial Intelligence. The gig economy undermines the notion of hierarchy and the meaning of a "job", although problems persist around exploitation and working conditions. Individualised career maps replace discrete career "ladders". The absence of standardised job descriptions and progression pathways leads to arbitrariness, confusion, and further atomisation.

Career maps give our managers discretion with little accountability or clarity to guide affirmative action. Bias is implicit in career development and promotion because managers *homosocialise*, or to put it another way, "birds of a feather flock together" (Elliot & Smith, 2004). Given the difficulty of monitoring and comparing career progression across organisations with open and flexible approaches to progression, unfairness and injustice are hidden and even more difficult to monitor and challenge.

Where next? I believe it is healthier to recognise our biases rather than deny them and how they shape our humanity. Perhaps it is the shame of accepting our flaws that leads to there being no proven link between recognising our biases and revising them? Researchers have found that racists armed with greater self-awareness only become worried about their behaviour and instead withdraw from encounters with other racial groups for fear of being offensive. The current trend for *Unconscious Bias* training in organisations is a positive thing if it gets us talking about difference. Yet, introspective sessions that merely nudge managers and employees into recognising – with an accompanying sense of shame – that they *are* biased becomes a distraction from the embedded, and structural disadvantages built into the workplace (Noon, 2018). We will forever wrestle with more or less transparent ways to re-distribute privilege in our social worlds, and in Chapter 7 I address in more detail our hypernormal attitudes to power in the workplace. In the next section I want to consider how we organise ourselves in the workplace, and identify alternatives to the scientifically informed hierarchy (Box 2.1, and see next).

Box 2.1 The informal clan resists neoliberalism

Interesting solutions emerge at a time when empowerment for women means competing for insecure and precarious employment in the marketplace. Female and male sales representatives selling generic medicines for rival pharmaceutical companies in a major European city decided to cooperate rather than compete. Unbeknownst to their managers – all male – workers from rival companies regularly met over lunch to discuss how they would divide their sales territories and redistribute their work. By cooperating as opposed to competing, everyone kept his or her jobs, and the fabric of society at the local level was maintained through balancing the work of production with reproduction. Growth remained at an acceptable level for the companies concerned, family-run restaurants prospered, and family work continued without the disruption that would inevitably accompany unemployment and relocation.

Organisational culture

Ecologies of the workplace. Organisational culture and climate are ideas that blur into each other. Research into *climate* goes back as far as the 1960s and focuses on what we can understand about an organisation from its written policies, practices, and procedures. I say more about this in the context of the *Corruption Complex* in Chapter 7. The study of *culture*, on the other hand, is more recent and tries to understand intangible things like shared perceptions and taken-for-granted assumptions about how groups understand, think, and react at a fundamental, perhaps pre-conscious, level of awareness (see Chapter 6). Culture talks about tribes, villages, histories, traditions and subcultures that merge and blur into the whole, or *gestalt* of an organisation. The critical function of culture is to create a distinctive identity for its members so they can tell themselves apart from others. It helps us shape how we engage with each other, learn from our mistakes, promote team-working, share values and influence the overall objectives of our organisations. We instinctively understand that the workplace contains more than one type of culture, or "them and us" subgroups, or cliques that we move smoothly through, between, around or within. Organisations are invested in promoting certain cultures because it is thought that staff who sign up to their values, mission statements, etc. become self-managing and cost less to motivate and monitor. Senior managers and leaders believe that culture is amenable to manufacture, and can be created in a top-down fashion. However, cultures are in fact spontaneous, ever-evolving, and largely beyond the ken of senior management, which is bad news for business schools (Grey, 2005).

Organisational culture results from the unintended, emergent consequences of two competing dimensions interacting with one another, namely: who is

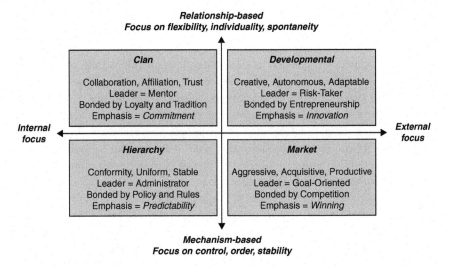

Figure 2.2 The competing values of organisational cultures.

the organisation for, and how much control can leaders exert to achieve their goals (Figure 2.2)? Organisation representatives will focus their attention on the development and wellbeing of people either *internally* or *externally*; although the boundaries are blurred, the former might look like a school, university, or hospital, for example, while the latter might be an insurance company. The target population for an organisation also influences its need for *control*, which aligns with predictability, stability, and hierarchy on the one hand, but rigidity, reporting failures, and missed opportunities on the other. *Flexibility*, meanwhile, a much-prized characteristic in the knowledge economy, is about a responsive, agile, and innovative workforce. The intersection of these four variables (i.e. *external/ internal* masters and *controlling/flexible systems of management*) creates a quadrant model (Box 2.2. *Clan, Developmental, Hierarchical*, and *Market*) for thinking about our different and often coexistent organisational cultures at work.

The story is, of course, more complicated than this because, quite astonishingly, researchers are only just beginning to acknowledge the head and heart dimension of an organisation's culture. This is about the importance of such things as the idealism, compassion, and personal meaning invested in the things we come together to do (Grabowski *et al.*, 2015). I say more about this in our final chapter, but for many of us, work is not just about our search for daily bread, but for our very meaning.

Box 2.2 Workplace ecologies

- The *clan* culture is typically characterised by an inward-looking stance, having at its core the belief that the organisation trusts in its commitment. This in turn is reciprocated through a cohesive, securely attached team ethos (see Chapter 6). Clans possess high morale and strong ethical working practices along with a deep sense of satisfaction and team commitment.

- A *developmental culture* is outward-looking, and values both personal and professional growth, autonomy, creativity, and risk-taking. Success is measured through innovation and cutting-edge outputs.

- *Hierarchies* focus on minimising anxiety through internal control. At their core is a lack of trust in people and resources. The core assumption is that predictability and stability lead to efficiency. Hierarchical cultures also value precise or even over-communication, conformity, routine, and consistency.

- *Market cultures* have an external focus and assume that achievement is measured through competitiveness, aggressiveness, productivity, and shareholder value. The most fundamental belief is that clear goals and money are sufficient to motivate performance. Things like beating competitors, improving product quality, and enhancing market share are measures of success.

A study of over 10,000 companies reveals that organisations do not exist as a single culture, but instead consist of a complex and dynamic blend of multiple intersecting and interacting cultures complementing each other and evolving over time (Hartnell *et al.*, 2011). Perhaps unsurprisingly, it is found that organisations with a strong market culture are rubbish at the business of caring and compassion. Their inability to be *nice* to their customers can, however, be ameliorated when a clan culture, which emphasises collaboration, trust, and support, is encouraged to participate in the business (van Beek & Gerritsen, 2010). Both *hierarchical* and *market* cultures have increased in popularity at the expense of *clans* in UK healthcare settings, for example, a process reflecting the marketization of care (Jacobs *et al.*, 2013). The importance of these and similar studies is that culture, even within large organisations, is not separate from but is shaped by context. This should not surprise us, as the boundaries between the workplace and the outside world are permeable, like the walls of a cell in symbiotic relationship with its environment.

In conclusion, the workplace contains a blend of cultures which if ignored or neglected becomes dominated by the prevailing cultural climate. In contemporary market-driven societies this means the atomising chill wind of neoliberalism blowing through our organisations. If the humanising clan and developmental cultures are acknowledged, understood, and nurtured, then with self-awareness and wisdom an organisation can support groups and teams become stewards of their own relational environment, thereby fostering the conditions for their members to flourish (Box 2.1 and 2.3).

Cultural ecologies and configurations of self. The idea that an organisation simultaneously exists as several dynamic and interacting cultures mirrors how the humanistic *Relational Approach* helps us integrate the often-contradictory facets of what it is to be a person. Configurations describe coherent patterns of feelings, thoughts, and behavioural responses that help us manage all manner of situations in our lives. Thinking about identity as configurations offers us a more sophisticated way of responding to the diverse and often contradictory external demands and internal imperatives that people face. Drawing on the example from earlier in the chapter (i.e., p28), suppose some *Unconscious Bias* training alerted me to a secret prejudice. I could deny that such shame-worthy attitudes define who I am, and simply avoid situations where my secret could be unwittingly revealed. Alternatively, I may accept this shadowy configuration of myself that feels uncomfortable with people who are unlike me. Acknowledging the part of me that fears what I do not understand helps me to accommodate the contradiction that I also think of myself as an accepting person. Allowing the shadowy, anxious configuration to live alongside the kinder one who acknowledges, and more importantly resists his shadow rescues me from insanity and may even lead to some personal development (Mearns & Thorne 2000, p. 116). Understanding organisational culture as an ecosystem mirrors configurations, because rather than inviting denial, awareness of complexity and conflict can furnish creative opportunities that may otherwise be missed. Giving voice to different self-concepts or cultures helps us to assimilate internal conflicts rather than split them off or project them elsewhere (see *Projections* and *Splitting*, Chapter 7). Through a non-defensive approach to both our personal and organisational contradictions, we avoid "zero-sum" interpretations, whereby for me (or the organisation) to win, someone else has to lose. In the example provided in Box 2.1, an informal clan of sales representatives recognises that for everyone to win, the contradictions of both collaboration and competition had to be assimilated so that a solution to the problems of the prevailing market culture was found.

Box 2.3 Reflective Exercise 1. *Cultural ecologies at work*

Consider the context in which you work. How many of the cultures in Box 2.2 can you see around you? Perhaps you belong to a group of peers who already offer you your main source of direction, support, inspiration, and feedback? If you belong to a team that is part of a market-based hierarchy, does your line manager seek to control what you do, and how you behave? Is your organisational setting about winning and competing? Does it pay attention to key performance indicators, and is the competition external, internal, or both? Are there elements of your organisation that seek to take risks and be innovative? Is there conflict here with the market-focused hierarchy that seeks a return on investment, and is uncomfortable with unpredictability? How does your organisation accommodate all these different parts? Which culture do you feel most comfortable with? Which, if any, raises strong feelings of belonging and connection for you?

Learning to work at the cultural boundaries. A tried and tested approach to cultivating reflectivity and self-awareness in organisations is *Appreciative Inquiry* (AI; Trajkovski *et al.*, 2013). It adopts a positive perspective, focusing on strengths as opposed to problems that only sustain discord (Cooperrider *et al.*, 2008). The first phase of *discovery* invites people to identify the best things about their organisation. The second phase is of *dreaming*, which imagines what the organisation might look like if the best things about it became the new *normal*. Taken together, these processes help identify clear goals for the subsequent *design* and *delivery* stages (Mills *et al.*, 2013). The lessons learnt through

AI are not easy listening for hard-driving competitive (*market*), bureaucratic, or controlling leaders and managers (*hierarchy*) in the compassion business who attempt to control structures from the "top down". Working with the sick and the dying is notoriously associated with high levels of surface acting, compassion fatigue, and burnout. An AI by healthcare professionals uncovered how oppressive hierarchical management, dispassionate role models, and a lack of support for reflection extinguished the flame of self-compassion and worker wellbeing (Curtis *et al.*, 2017). As we shall see later, organisations in the compassion business can nurture both *clan* and *developmental* cultures through democratising relationships (Chapter 5). Trusting both clan and developmental cultures requires we acknowledge that workers understand that we do not live in a utopian world of limitless resources, and that we can be accountable for what we spend and how we spend it. Should you remain unconvinced by the problem with market-driven bureaucratic hierarchies, then please, indulge me for a little longer.

The problem is … I'm too busy to listen … or reflect! The most persistent complaint of the bureaucratic command-and-control leadership model is that it is dehumanising and paradoxically inefficient, especially in the context of the business of caring for others (de Zulueta, 2015). The machine metaphor invites the myth of control, assumes linear causation, and focuses on the object-ification of human beings rather than on a deeper engagement in relationships. The *market* culture, especially, instrumentalises and objectifies people and our interactions with each other. We stop recognising ourselves in our own works, and instead become estranged and alienated from one another. The exercise I describe in Box 2.4 (*I'm too busy to listen – is it OK if I fake it?*) was developed in response to a genuine and, I think, reasonable question posed during a well-being training course I facilitated. It is an attempt to answer the question as well as foster a sense of authentic concern for the wellness of a fellow human being in the context of work. When we truly listen, a person can tell you about himself or herself, what really troubles them, and perhaps even how they can find their own solutions.

Academics challenge the notion that organisations involved in the compassion business, knowledge management, and high-end technology have at their core equally sophisticated levels of reflection. The truth does not sit easily with the outward appearance of seeming *smart*. Irrationality and a rigid adherence to wishful thinking supports the myth of certainty and predictability, especially in hierarchal cultures where skilled incompetence means real problems are either avoided or ignored. This is not a criticism; busy people do the best they can to make reasonable or acceptable decisions in the time they believe available. Mats Alvesson and André Spicer coined the provocative term *functional stupidity* (2012) – not to be confused with cognitive impairment, incompetence, or irrationality – to describe unreflective compliance and decision-making, which I believe is driven by a need to defend against difficult emotions such as anxiety, fear, and shame. Hierarchies, Alvesson argues, are simply intolerant of authenticity and vulnerability. An organisation uses *functional stupidity* to defend itself against frightening self-doubt, uncertainty, and the inability to justify structures and actions (see Bion's *Basic Assumptions*, in Chapter 6). Reflectivity risks raising doubt among leaders and managers about their legitimacy and undermines their commitment to potentially dubious courses of action. Although *functional stupidity* may be necessary to the internal workings of an organisation, it nevertheless has the negative effect of ensnaring people into distorted or incongruent ways of both thinking and being. When doubt is thrown on the meaning of our working life, it threatens a downward spiral toward cynicism, alienation, decreased motivation, and detachment. When this happens, we defend ourselves by retreating into ways of thinking and feeling that distract us from potentially identity-threatening and uncertainty-inducing consequences. This self-reinforcing loop of functional stupidity elicits even more illusory certainty.

A similarly provocative observation on the problem of (*functional*) stupidity in hierarchies was made by the soldier Kurt von Hammerstein-Equord (1878–1943), who felt he could divide his officers into four groups: clever, industrious, lazy, and the (*functionally*) stupid. Each one, he believed, usually possessed two of these qualities. The clever and industrious were appointed to the highest level of his staff. The officer who was clever and lazy was suited to high leadership positions because they had the requisite intellectual clarity and composure to make difficult decisions. Under certain circumstances, use could be made of those who were (*functionally*) stupid and lazy, because they were less likely to do harm. Yet the (*functionally*) stupid and industrious "must be got rid of", for they were far too dangerous.

A fundamental assumption about the market hierarchy is that we use control as a proxy for trust. When structures grow beyond a certain critical mass of, say, a clan, we can no longer rely on being heard, have our dilemmas understood without judgement, or be sure that strangers have reflected carefully on actions that affect us. We do not trust we are valued for who we are beyond the economic transaction of our contracts or positions in the hierarchy. At the heart of a *Relational Approach* is trust, and we cannot go further without considering the types of contract which enshrine such trust in the workplace.

Box 2.4 Too busy to listen – is it OK if I fake it?

At least three people are required for this exercise (see *The Triad Method*, Chapter 4, for more details). It can be carried out sitting or standing, with the latter resembling our informal encounters.

The *speaker* briefly (3–5 minutes) describes some challenge they are facing at work. Choose an issue that is real and relevant to you, but not so sensitive that it requires a confidential setting.

Listener A is positioned at a slight angle to the speaker – close enough to hear what is being said, but not too close to feel intrusive. Their aim is to communicate *attending skills* to the speaker. They should seek to hold the speaker gently in their gaze, focusing on the bridge of the nose, or some point midway between the brows. Both non-verbal (i.e. nodding, positive facial expressions) and verbal (hmmm, uh-huh, I see, I hear what you are saying) encouragers are useful to let the speaker know that they are being heard. Along with active listening, you can also use sparingly, *OARS* micro-skills (see, Chapter 5, Box 5.2 for more details).

Listener B is also positioned alongside *Listener A*, at a slight angle to the *speaker*. They have the difficult task of avoiding the use of attending skills. This means they do not engage in eye contact or verbal and non-verbal encouragers. They can play with their phone, stare out the window, or perhaps work on their laptop (sound familiar?).

At the end of the exercise, *Listener B* de-briefs. What did you hear? What details of the speaker's story can you recall? Did you pick-up on any emotional content in their story? Now *Listener A* de-briefs. Does the experience of the two listeners differ? Are there any surprises? Did the content of what was heard differ? Finally, the *speaker* describes their experience of being heard and not-heard. Now swap roles and repeat.

Fairness is in the eye of the beholder

Our silent contracts. A legal contract is a formal, written-down thing negotiated and understood by those involved. It implies that those who are part of it have read and agreed to its terms and conditions. An employment contract, on the other hand rarely involves equal partners. Nor is it explicitly negotiated and agreed to in the same way that simpler ones are. In general, entering into a relationship with an employer means becoming junior to a more powerful authority. For example, the emotional labour when offered a job as a middle manager in a poorly led organisation is perhaps implied but rarely made explicit. This is because the employment relationship is suffused with the ambiguity of implicit and unspecified expectations. It is an informal, dynamic social process and not a static one-off economic transaction as implied when we buy something like a toaster. To illustrate the point, consider one of the most potent weapons in the armoury of a Trade Union, which is working to rule. Here, workers can cause huge disruption to the employer by merely agreeing to follow to the letter their contract or job description. If following the rules of a written contract can be so disruptive, how can it fully define the working relationship? Denise Rousseau (1995) recognised the ambiguity of work as a social process through the idea of the psychological contract. It helps us understand work in terms of relationships that unfold in usually unnoticed ways that is strongly influenced by our personal biases, emotional histories, anxieties, fears, and what we feel entitled to. The psychological contract influences the relationship as it unfolds over time, from the preparation of a role specification and when the prospective worker reads the job advert. Rousseau recognised two forms of psychological contract:

- *Relational* types are open-ended, often long-term, and as such require ongoing tweaking informed by good faith, ideas of fairness, values, mutual support, and inter-dependency. It has been shown that when we can convey a strong sense of fairness, virtue, and transparency in the workplace, employee commitment and turnover are improved (Huhtala & Feldt, 2016). So research supports the old adage: *people leave managers, not jobs.*
- *Transactional* arrangements are unfortunately increasingly popular in the neoliberal economy. Work tends to have a fixed, short-term duration with a narrow focus on a clearly defined outcome. Commitment and security tends to be low on both sides. Whilst the transactional can evolve into the relational, the popularity of short-term arrangements has led to a fragmentation of the workforce and an erosion of organisational memory, good faith, perceptions of fairness, and ethical behaviour.

The unspoken nature of our psychological contracts means they are largely silent until one or other party casually, carelessly, or furtively changes something. The elusive nature of our unspoken expectations means that it is often difficult to explain how or why our contracts are either *breached* or more seriously *violated*. The former occurs when a perceived imbalance or inequity in the psychological contract comes into awareness for employer or employee. For example, a large company based on the edge of town decides to introduce parking charges, with the fee set as a percentage of employee income. There may be good reasons for doing this at an organisational level, but workers may see this change as an unjust *breach* of their psychological contract because up until that point, it was assumed that free parking was a benefit of employment.

The very perception of unfairness at work has a profound negative impact on employee psychological wellbeing. Feeling strongly about some change indicates that we have gone beyond a contract *breach*, and are now in the serious domain of a *violation*. We may not always recognise at a cognitive level when a breach occurs, but we *feel* strongly about violations. Staying with the car-parking scenario, anger among ordinary employees, a sense of betrayal and industrial action quickly follow when it emerges that the salary-indexed parking fees are to be capped below the pay of the best-off senior managers in the organisation. A sense of injustice develops into outrage when it appears, quite justifiably, that workers are being exploited.

The hierarchical culture often views the expectations of workers as maladjusted and problematic. For managers who believe their decisions – about parking charges, for example – are based on a rational appraisal of economic factors, breaches and violations of psychological contracts are seen as resistance by workers (or unions) who want only to maintain the status quo. For workers it is a different and simpler story: managers fail to keep their promises and commitments. The difficulty lies partly in contemporary employment relations, where managers are increasingly intolerant of time-consuming collective bargaining. With the rise of neoliberal values, informal arrangements are more useful to managers because promises can be readily made and broken in response to the fast-moving business environment. Rather than attempt to rescue an acrimonious and failing project, I propose that it is much simpler to examine our silent contracts before embarking on the enterprise (Box 2.5).

Box 2.5 Reflective Exercise 2. *Exploring the silent contract*

Consider a project or task where you will be working with several others.

- What are your unshared hopes?
- What do you imagine to be the unplanned outcomes?
- What prevents you from sharing these aspirations?
- What fantasies do you have about the unspoken ambitions of others?
- Do you imagine that others also share these blocks?
- In exploring these unspoken ideas and fantasies, are there any actions you would now consider taking?

Justice at work. Our individual sense of justice lies at the heart of our silent contracts. We develop our own belief in what is fair recognition for our labour at work by balancing inputs with outcomes. The former broadly entitle me to the latter, and can include obvious things like effort, time, skill, and compliance. However, it also extends to how far I am willing to tolerate compromises to my values and integrity, i.e. how much incongruence can I survive? *Outcomes*, on the other hand, include a balance between financial rewards, job security, stability, esteem, a social network, pensions, and health care. If I feel that the balance is out of kilter, then we may adjust our input to re-establish some sense of equilibrium. In addition to this narrow, transactional concept of fairness, our sense of equity can be seen as a set of broader social practices in the workplace. Perceived injustices around how rewards are shared (*distributive*), decision-making processes are conducted (*procedural*), and how we are treated by others (*relational*) all have the potential to seriously undermine our psychological wellbeing, and the likelihood we will absent ourselves from the workplace (Box 2.6; Ndjaboué *et al.*, 2012).

Box 2.6 Reflective Exercise 3. *How fair is your workplace?*

Consider how fair your workplace feels in terms of:

Distributive justice
- Do you feel the stress in your job is worth the effort?
- Is your salary fair compared to the efforts of your colleagues?

Procedural justice
  Are procedures in your workplace designed to:

- Hear the concerns of all those affected by decision-making?
- Provide opportunities to appeal or challenge a decision?

Relational justice
- Do you feel criticised unfairly or appropriately praised for your work?

How do we deny the disruptive power of the silent contact? It is all too easy for busy people to believe that we do not have the time to clarify the boundaries of arrangements we make in our everyday working lives. Unless we can give attention to even the most obvious details, misunderstandings and assumptions can occur, leading to perceived breaches, violations, wasted time, and emotional labour further down the line. You may already be familiar with some of the tell-tale "get-out clauses" or phrases that we use with others, or hear used on us when communicating our levels of commitment to some arrangement or project:

- **I will try ...** (*but expect to fail*) and get back to you next Tuesday.
- **I think I will ...** (*but not sure I can*) make it a priority.

- **I should ...** (*but probably won't*) follow this up with an email.
- **I can ...** (*but may not*) put this on my list of things to do.
- **I will work on it ...** (*but doubt I will succeed*) before our next meeting.
- **I will take a look ...** (*but not sure when*) at this ... leave it with me.

In common with what underpins effective psychotherapy, clear, precise, and inclusive contracting creates a strong working alliance. It ensures an open and transparent process without hidden agendas. People are *included* in decisions that affect them, they are more likely to commit to change, and it helps all parties know when the work is complete. We return to goal-oriented relationships in Chapter 5, but here I want to outline a useful framework for denying the powerful forces of competing psychological contracts in the workplace (Box 2.7).

Box 2.7 Denying the disruptive power of our psychological contracts

- *Who will be involved?* If someone important has not been invited at the beginning, there may be difficulties when completing the task down the line.
- *What will these people do?* Precision about who will be accountable for which aspects of a project – especially when many people are involved – is an obvious but important thing to agree at the outset.
- *How long will it take?* If deadlines are driven by external factors then there may be little flexibility. However obvious it may be to some, stating and writing down agreements about timings is essential.
- *What is our goal?* Contracts invariably flounder when there is a lack of clarity about the goal. Classically, goals must be Specific, Measurable, Attainable, Realistic, and Timely (SMART). However, when there are too many competing goals, energy for the project becomes diffuse. All involved must be clear about how a transparent contract will benefit them, so to promote trust, openness, energy, and motivation.
- *How will we recognise when the task or process is finished?* If it is difficult to measure or it is intangible then all must agree to re-visit this on a regular basis.
- *How will we mark the end of the contract?* When a project simply fizzles out, people become demotivated and feel that their investment of time and energy have not been recognised. It is important that all contributions are valued, prized, and celebrated.

Things to keep in mind

- We arrive in the world of work with a good part of our *worldview* already in place. It has the dual role of helping us navigate our environment, yet it potentially undermines our wellbeing and limits how we engage with others.
- The organisational ecology in which we find ourselves is an array of intersecting and interacting subcultures which, when approached with self-awareness, offers a potentially sophisticated approach for responding to internal imperatives and external demands.
- Clear and inclusive contracting ensures transparency because it denies the powerful forces of our silent contracts. An eye for detail, an appreciation of context, and well-developed listening skills facilitate effective contracting and encourages trust.

References

Acker J. (2012). Gendered organizations and intersectionality: problems and possibilities. *Equality, Diversity and Inclusion: An International Journal*, 31(3), 214–224.

Alvesson M & Spicer A. (2012). A stupidity-based theory of organizations. *Journal of Management Studies*, 49(7), 1194–1220.

Bal M. (2017). *Dignity in the workplace: New theoretical perspectives*. Basingstoke: Palgrave Macmillan.

van Beek APA & Gerritsen DL. (2010). The relationship between organizational culture of nursing staff and quality of care for residents with dementia. *International Journal of Nursing Studies*, 47, 1274–1282.

Britton DM & Logan L. (2008). Gendered organisations: progress and prospects. *Sociology Compass*, 2(1), 107–121.

Cooperrider DL, Whitney D, & Stavros J. (2008). *Appreciative inquiry handbook* (2nd ed.). Brunswick, OH: Crown Custom Publishing.

Curtis K, Gallagher A, Ramage C, Montgomery J, Martin C, Leng J, … Wrigley M. (2017). Using appreciative inquiry to develop, implement and evaluate a multi-organisation "Cultivating Compassion" programme for health professionals and support staff. *Journal of Research in Nursing*, 22(1–2), 150–165.

Diefenbach T. (2019). Why Michels' 'iron law of oligarchy' is not an iron law – and how democratic organisations can stay "oligarchy-free". *Organization Studies*, 40(4), 545–562.

Eisenstein H. (2017). Hegemonic feminism, neoliberalism and womenomics: "empowerment" instead of liberation? *New Formations: A Journal of Culture, Theory & Politics*, 91, 35–49.

Elliot J & Smith R. (2004). Race, gender and workplace power. *American Sociological Review*, 69, 365–86.

Fine C. (2017). *Testosterone Rex: Unmaking the myths of our gendered minds*. London: Icon Books Ltd.

Grabowski L, Neher C, Crim T, & Mathiassen L. (2015). Competing values framework application to organizational effectiveness in voluntary organizations: A case study. *Nonprofit and Voluntary Sector Quarterly*, 44(5), 908–923.

Grech V. (2015). Evidence of economic deprivation and female foeticide in a United Nations global births by gender data set. *Early Human Development*, 91, 855–858.

Grey C. (2005). *A very short, fairly interesting and reasonably cheap book about studying organizations.* London: Sage.

Hartnell CA, Ou AY, & Kinicki A. (2011). Organizational culture and organizational effectiveness: A meta-analytic investigation of the competing values framework's theoretical suppositions. *Journal of Applied Psychology*, 96(4), 677–694.

Huhtala M & Feldt T. (2016). The path from ethical organisational culture to employee commitment: Mediating roles of value congruence and work engagement. *Scandinavian Journal of Work and Organizational Psychology*, 1(3), 1–14.

Jacobs R, Mannion R, Davies HTO, Harrison S, Konteh F, & Walsh K. (2013). The relationship between organizational culture and performance in acute Hospitals. *Social Science & Medicine*, 76, 115–125.

Marx K & Engels F. (1977). *The German ideology*, Ed. CJ Arthur. London: Lawrence & Wishart.

Mearns D & Thorne B. (2000). *Person-centred therapy today. New frontiers in theory and practice.* London: Sage.

Merquior JG. (1986). *Western Marxism.* London: Paladin.

Mills MJ, Fleck CR, & Kozikowski A. (2013). Positive psychology at work: a conceptual review, state-of-practice assessment, and a look ahead. *The Journal of Positive Psychology*, 8(2), 153–164.

Ndjaboué R, Brisson C, & Vézina M. (2012). Organisational justice and mental health: a systematic review of prospective studies. *Occupational and Environmental Medicine*, 69(10), 694–700.

Noon M. (2018). Pointless diversity training: Unconscious bias, new racism and agency. *Work, Employment and Society*, 32(1) 198–209.

Pusey M. (1987). *Jürgen Habermas: Key sociologists series* (Ed. Peter Hamilton). London: Tavistock.

Rousseau D. (1995). *Psychological contracts in organisations: Understanding the written and unwritten Agreements.* London: Sage.

Taylor FW. (1911). *The principles of scientific management.* New York: Harper and Brothers.

Trajkovski S, Schmied V, Vickers M, & Jackson D. (2013). Implementing the 4D cycle of appreciative inquiry in health care: A methodological review. *Journal of Advanced Nursing*, 69(6), 1224–1234.

de Zulueta PC. (2015). Developing compassionate leadership in health care: An integrative review. *Journal of Healthcare Leadership*, 8, 1–10.

Chapter 3

A matter of survival

Not at the table? You could be on the menu

Expanding my menu of options. When reflecting on our relationships at work, we must confront the unavoidable truth that they all involve sometimes quite powerful emotions. When things are going well, work can be an exhilarating experience where we feel warmth, acceptance, of tremendous value and worth, pride, and even gratitude. As many of us meet our partners through work, we must also include feelings of sexual attraction and of course falling in love. Then there is also the dark side: anger in all its various presentations, including frustration, feeling pissed off, annoyed, and even the passive type that I discuss in Chapter 7. Jealousy, despair, hopelessness, regret, rejection, sadness, and contempt are some of the ingredients that go to make work such a human business. Such sensations do not happen in isolation, of course. In addition to how *we* feel, we should also be alert to the dynamic relationship we have with our environment and context. By this, I mean that the way *others* react to my emotional world has both a positive and negative impact on the quality of our ongoing relationship. For example, if I throw caution to the wind and show how angry I am with a colleague, then I potentially invite all sorts of stereotypical behaviour towards me, such as retaliation, distancing, or even attempts to draw closer to offer comfort. My capacity to appropriately manage – or modulate – my emotional response towards those around me is termed *affect regulation*, and is another way of thinking about the emotional labour we do, which I introduced in the previous chapter. Those of us who possess a broad repertoire of emotional responses to others in times of stress are more flexible when we encounter new or unexpected situations, such as when somebody gets angry. When our menu of choices is limited, we use familiar strategies that are less successful for getting our relational needs met. Research clearly shows that relationships that are supportive, non-judgemental and respectful help us expand our menu of emotional responses to new, stressful or, as we examine next, even dangerous situations.

Working with the big three: *Fear, Anger,* **and** *Shame.* Danger is so normal and universal in our world that over millennia our brains have evolved systems or strategies to help us survive (Crittenden, 2012). Protecting ourselves from actual or anticipated danger takes priority over those other basic human needs such as belonging, approval, esteem, and sexual intimacy (Maslow, 1999, p. 220). Both at work and beyond, we can only engage in developing our talents and capacities when we feel we are free from actual or anticipated danger. The dangers in our mind that we protect ourselves from in the present have at their root strategies (explored later) developed to stay safe during childhood. Importantly, the big three emotions, as I call them, are at the heart of our survival strategies which are, respectively; *flee, attack,* or *flop (freeze),* which kick in when we are surprised by some threat.

I am especially grateful to my *fear* response because without it I would not have survived an unexpected attack by a hippopotamus. She in her turn, I expect, was fearful or even angry at my presence in her territory. As the pool exploded in a frenzy of white foam and pink gaping jaw just yards from where I was walking, my reaction was spontaneous. I fled for my life without a moment's pause to think it through. My all-encompassing bodily reaction to the danger soon subsided, though, after the threat had passed and I was sure I was safe. Now if the workplace is relatively free of agitated semiaquatic herbivores, what is it that we fear or feel anxious about when at work?

While solitude has its place in human experience, a cavernous feeling of separation looms when we see no human connection in prospect. A fundamental desire to avoid danger underpins our social nature, meaning we seek out others to connect with and stay safe. Ironically, this brings with it the accompanying anxiety of rejection by those we rely on for safety. Anxiety is related to fear in that it has a similar physiological effect on our bodies, yet it differs in that it is a longer-lasting, chronic experience characterised by the anticipation of some threat, danger, or harm in the future (Pavuluri *et al.*, 2002). Having been driven to clamber aboard our metaphorical *social life rafts* in a sea of perceived danger and uncertainty, we then experience the anxiety of rejection by those who offer us succour. In short, our anxiety about being at the table is in tension with our fear of being on the menu.

Let us be more concrete about the role of *fear and anxiety* at work. The planned obsolescence intrinsic to our consumer-driven neoliberal economies stalks the corridors of our organisations. What happens if I underperform in an organisation already full of objects we do not need? Typically, fearful experiences at work might include conflict with a figure of authority who we rely on for employment, rejection (i.e. ostracism: Chapter 7), restructuring, rightsizing, streamlining, dehiring, delayering, outplacing, or indeed any practice that makes our environment feel less safe and predictable.

Anger is very much an internal event like any other emotion, and signals that something is going wrong in our environment. If expressed clearly, anger can be instructive, not destructive. We usually talk-down anger though, speaking instead of our *frustration* with a colleague or a situation, feeling *pissed off*, or to use the polite euphemism, finding people or situations *challenging*, code for the emotional labour of not losing it. Like our angry herbivore who is looking for a fight, overt anger at work can be a response to some perceived threat to our "territory", authority, or rank. Much more common, however, is the covert anger that I explore in the context of emotional aggression in Chapter 7.

If we are not in a position to flee or fight, then *flop* becomes our most powerful involuntary response to managing situations where our status in the world is at risk, threatened or devalued. It relates to *shame*, and how we hope others will see us: "How valuable am I? How desirable am I? Am I worthy of being liked, or promoted, never mind loved? Do you even want me here?" As social animals, negative self-evaluations of any of these questions understandably evoke fear and pain, which is why some of the cruellest examples of emotional abuse in the workplace includes ostracism and scapegoating (Chapter 7). The submissive, "floppy" posture of shame, with eyes downcast and shoulders slumped, links to the survival extinct of *freezing* which some of you may be able to relate to from childhood (Box 3.1). Here we seek to disarm the threat of predation through an avoidant posture or coy and embarrassed smile, which signals: *just go away and leave me alone* (Gilbert & Andrews, 1998). Perhaps the shame we feel is in recognition of the fact that we do actually need other people, which then ironically gets in the way of tolerating those with whom our wellbeing is entangled. The prospect of being exposed, scrutinised, or negatively judged also evokes visceral fear. We can make the case that shame is not so much about simply falling short of some idealised self, but being too close to our dreaded and shameful undesired self, a state of being similar to the Rogerian notion of incongruence.

In short, what I would call the big three emotions of fear, anger, and shame fuel our organising strategies for fleeing, attacking, or flopping when surprised by some threat or danger. These emotions can be overwhelming and literally sensational, blocking our ability to think and reflect, driving us to stumble blindly over friends and colleagues who want to help. When unacknowledged and unchecked, they become problematic as they undermine how we relate to others, and vice versa. The importance of learning to regulate and tolerate the big three emotions cannot be overstated, especially in the contexts in which we now live and work. The emotions behind survival and natural selection are powerful, but I also trust in our powers to reason and reflect, which can be just as formidable in exerting their own selection pressures. As we shall see shortly, although we develop our strategies in childhood, they need not be immutable (Box 3.1).

Box 3.1 The stone in his shoe

The line of classmates snaked round three corners of the room, with all eyes fixed unblinkingly on the teacher. "No, no, no ..." she barks, the exasperation all too evident by the veins on her temple: "Start again with you Esme ... now ... seven fives are ... ?" Esme responds confidently: "thirty-five", and so the creeping wave of shame begins its inexorable, terrifying journey round the room towards me. "Let's see, eleven others to go, we switch to the sixes at Maxine, so that makes me five times ... erm, oh no, what's happened now?" The wave has halted at Lee, who stutters: "I don't know Sister Mary!" He stands, head bowed, shoulders slumped, and eyes cast down, unable to think, frozen to the spot. He wants to run, but he can't. A whisper and a nudge from a kind classmate risks the wrath of Sister Mary, but she gives him the answer anyway: "fifty-five ..." he stammers, and the wave of shame creeps on. Lee was taught a lesson in fear and shame, which he carries around like a stone in his shoe to this day.

Who do you trust? I do not assume that the past is more powerful than the present, but I do believe that the strategies we develop for dealing with dangerous or unpleasant situations in the past may not always be appropriate for our present. So this is why I wish to pose some questions, to begin exploring the importance of *trust* to you, especially in our working relationships (Box 3.2). Trust is especially poignant and arguably in short supply in the context of management bureaucracies because at their core is an unstated anxiety about our capacity to trust others to give us what we need. And getting what we need is critical to our survival from the moment we enter the world and instinctively nuzzle for our mother's nipple.

Box 3.2 Attachment figures in the workplace

- Does someone at work remind you of a teacher, relative, or some other significant figure from the past who had the knack of making you feel safe?
- In times of stress, who do you automatically go to for advice? On the other hand, are there others you would avoid? Do you expect them to have some ulterior motive in their dealings with you?
- How much do you trust your manager? Do *they* require constant vigilance?
- If you lead others, how does it feel to have them depend on you? Do you prefer to let people sort things out for themselves? Do you find "needy" colleagues suffocating or irritating.

Danger and attachment

Managing our relationship with danger. John Bowlby was amongst the first to draw attention to the way that from infancy, our relationships are reciprocal, dynamic, and evolving as opposed to being static and one-way. In other words, new-borns are much more than doubly incontinent eating machines; we are survival geniuses who actively co-create our relationship with caregivers to have our needs met. The growth spurt of a breast-fed baby, for example, is a noisy and sometimes painful "invitation" to increase mum's milk supply. The attuned mother in her turn seeks to meet the exhausting demands of her actively involved infant through more regular nursing.

Attachment theory is a lifespan theory that applies to all our important relationships and contexts, and is relevant from the moment of our birth up to the last moments of life when we finally lose our battle with avoiding danger (Landa & Duschinsky, 2013). Death matters so much to us precisely because of our attachment to life. To understand the role of attachment theory in the social process of work, we must first consider how the big three emotions shape our relationships in infancy.

From the cradle ... From the moment we are born we absorb, transform, and make sense of information about the potential dangers in our environment. The relational strategies we develop as infants and beyond are not formal cognitive plans created through some conscious analysis. A balanced strategy for an infant who does not feel particularly endangered, for example, combines *both* protest about a momentary absence of their carer, with the ability to be soothed on their return. This strategy emerges especially when carers are consistent and attuned in relation to their infant, because they do not need to be coerced into being available to provide protection against danger. Far from being diabolical and destructive, fear, anger, and to some extent shame are essential emotions for keeping us safe in our earliest relationships. They are the tools we use to avoid danger in a world we cannot always trust to meet our needs.

Other less-balanced strategies for security seeking in times of stress develop because our carer is either consistently unreliable or unavailable. By managing our justifiable anger, rage, and fear, we learn to invite them back into contact with us. An unreliable carer, for example, is treated with alternating combinations of hysterical screaming, slapping, etc. (anger), and disarming clinginess. We will say more about these strategies of attachment in the next section, but first I want to convey to you how the relationship habits from our early years play out in the context of work.

... to the workplace. When we feel valued and trusted in the workplace, our sense of feeling secure is high because we feel safe. We feel confident about

expressing our thoughts and feelings openly and clearly, and are usually ready and indeed seek to negotiate compromises about what to do about problems. Yet when circumstances change and things feel risky, such as in times of restructuring, or when working with people we do not know who may not have our best interests at heart, we choose other, more guarded strategies. It would be guileless, after all, to let those we do not trust know what we are going to do, what we think, or what we feel. It could, after all, be the strategy that leads to the loss of our rank, job, and income.

Consider the impact of an influential figure in your organisation who appears to lose interest in you or the group you lead. If you felt *secure* in your relationship with this person or the organisation, then you might be confident in expressing how angry or worried you are about feeling abandoned. After all, in the context of work it could signal a dire threat to you or your team. If trust is absent, you adopt an alternative strategy, which is to *avoid* expressing your negative feelings. By hiding what you really feel, you avoid the risk of further rejection or even some punitive backlash against your perceived impertinence.

How about the manager who is well meaning but inconsistent? One minute they lavish you with their time and attention, and the next you are blanked. It is as if they felt *anxious* about being around you. Where do you stand? What have you done to invite the rejection? How do you get their attention back? Perhaps you adopt the strategy of coercive aggression. First, you work hard to please and flatter them, being a bit clingy and attention-seeking until they are interested in you again, at which point you express your anger. Naturally, in the context of work we are not openly angry but we use instead socially acceptable means to communicate our frustration, i.e. passive aggressive strategies such as ignoring or responding tardily to emails, and being late for or inattentive at meetings (Chapter 7). In effect, you punish your figure of authority for withdrawing their love.

The workplace is not a therapeutic environment and this book is not attempting to turn you into a psychotherapist. Yet work is where we most often seek to make sense of the big three emotions of fear, anger, and shame. In times of stress, we stop thinking and reflecting and instead process what is happening in the moment using memory systems from the past. It is possible to use more than one strategy, and we can use different strategies at different times depending on our environment and context. It is important to emphasise, however, that although our strategies are not random, we are not stuck with them forever. I want to emphasise that I am a world away from categorising people according to their default relationship strategies, which I explore further in the next part.

Attachment strategies

By observing infants with their carers, researchers noticed how ingenious we are at developing strategies for solving the problem of ensuring a safer environment for ourselves. I use the term *strategy* here as a shorthand for the characteristics of a relationship, including the patterns of expectations, emotions, and behaviours we employ when seeking to minimise risk. At the time of Mary Ainsworth's initial studies on attachment with middle-class families, two broad categories of behaviour were identified, namely *secure* (63%) and *insecure*, with the latter subdivided into *anxious* or *preoccupied* (16%) and *avoidant* (21%). The secure strategy is considered the default setting when we trust our environment. It is more interesting, however, to consider patterns for managing insecure or riskier situations.

- Carers who are *anxious*, preoccupied, or absent-minded are likely to create an equally anxious relationship with their infant. When an infant's needs are met tardily or unwillingly, or when they are perhaps regarded as something of a nuisance, they are likely to become apprehensive when seeking out their carer. The carer cannot be trusted to be available, responsive, or even physically there for that matter. To survive the uncertainty, we develop the strategy of clinging to our carer's side, remaining emotionally vigilant and watchful of non-verbal signals that they will leave. The strategy works by inviting the carer to be more available.
- The second approach is simply to shut down, suppress, or *avoid* difficult emotions. In certain situations, the "freeze and flop" response is a way to survive life-threatening or traumatic events. However, the child who cries and cries yet nobody comes begins to recognise that perhaps they are in fact abandoned. Shutting down as a strategy for surviving rejection is a way of managing hopelessness, and is likely to develop as a pattern of behaviour where avoidance competes with the desire for intimacy.
- A disputed fourth *disorganised* strategy emerged alongside the triad of *organised* systems (i.e. secure, anxious, and avoidant) which helps us understand severe levels of trauma and psychological distress (Holmes & Slade, 2018, chapter 10). *Fearful* attachment strategies are considered to be a severely avoidant way of relating to others, transmitted by trauma through the generations. A carer who *freezes* with fright in response to the distress of their infant does so because it triggers their own unprocessed fearful memories. The capacity to care becomes paralysed, leaving the infant vulnerable, alone, and terrified.

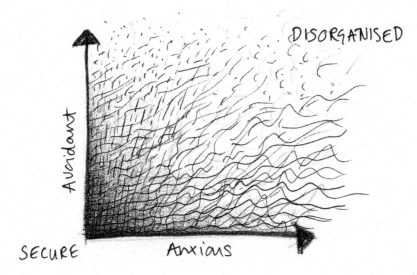

Figure 3.1 Relationship systems as continuum.

Disorganised attachment represents an extension of the continuum of organised strategies we develop as infants to help us survive. The strategies we employ as infants are sensible solutions for surviving the environment in which we find ourselves. We move along and throughout a continuum of strategies in response to our context, setting and relationship histories. However, the difficulty comes when we employ a particular survival strategy in an inappropriate context as an adult. For example, it is OK for a psychotherapist to employ an avoidant strategy when behind the wheel of their car as it ensures the safety of vulnerable road users. However, such a strategy is wildly inappropriate in the consulting room. I say more about choosing appropriate strategies next.

The strength of the pack is the wolf – and the strength of the wolf is the pack. Strong prejudices exist about how we form trusting relationships at work. The increasing popularity of online selection tools and other methods designed to engineer-out lone wolves during promotion or recruitment processes is a worrying development, the assumption being that attachment strategies are immutable and that secure ones alone are the healthiest and most desirable at work. However, trust and the way we relate to each other is a process. Any organisation genuinely committed to employee wellbeing must acknowledge that bureaucracies have at their core a systemic mistrust of its members, and this creates an insecure climate to *do* relationships.

Whilst secure strategies are useful when it comes to leading and coordinating activities and working with others to solve problems, they are not necessarily the most valuable in times of change and threat. As individuals, we are not so good at avoiding danger. As far as the natural world is concerned, we are slow, not terribly strong, and have a poor sense of smell and sight. We do not have claws or sharp teeth, and flying is out of the question. The main advantage we have is our ability to form groups. When being pursued by a snapping hippopotamus it is the slowest in the group who provides safety for the rest. Therefore, our attachment strategies reflect the diversity of responses we need to survive a hostile environment (Ein-Dor & Hirschberger, 2016). Those employing an *Avoidant* strategy are often characterised as having deactivated emotions useful for self-reliance and in teams they are the sentinels who watch out for risks and threats. Such strategies facilitate unintended trail-blazing, showing others the way to adapt or survive stressful situations, albeit by sheer coincidence. Selecting against neural diversity in its broadest sense undermines those organisations that seek to be innovative, creative, and most importantly, inclusive. All the more reason to be concerned, then, by homosocialisation, where people responsible for monitoring and controlling bureaucratic structures favour those like themselves irrespective of their attachment strategies.

Research on attachment and the workplace. Attachment theory has much to offer us about how we trust others, and how we form stable working relationships. It stresses how our interdependence and diversity is a strength and not a weakness. Yet in the 40 years since the idea of attachment first emerged, half of all research about its impact on the world of work has appeared in only the past decade (Yip *et al.*, 2018). Perhaps unsurprisingly, we are learning that people who default to *secure* strategies tend to worry less about their jobs, seeing their workplace in a positive way as evidenced through both their commitment and a willingness to focus on the interests of others first. They are also less likely to report that work interferes with their home life, and if anything they report a positive spill over between the two. Alternatively, people defaulting to *insecure* strategies are more likely to say that work, as opposed to home life, was more important to them in terms of their overall sense of wellbeing (Harms, 2011). *Anxious* strategies keep us in our jobs for longer, either because we fear being unable to find anything better, or because we believe that we will be unable to manage the disruption of leaving a job. Those using *avoidant* strategies, perhaps unsurprisingly, struggle to engage with both their organisation and colleagues (Byrne *et al.*, 2017). So, the interesting question is whether we deploy secure attachment strategies at work only by default, or must we firstly enjoy the benefits of a secure working environment before we reciprocate and trust others? Research shows that organisational representatives (i.e. managers) who work hard to create a trusting environment for their employees markedly improve levels of engagement. So, whilst there is clearly a correlation between our default attachment strategies and behaviour at work, *employees can and do adapt positively to the way organisational representatives conduct themselves* (Scrima et al., 2015).

A Relational Approach

The third force of humanism. Psychotherapists and counsellors already profit from attachment theory because it offers us a relational understanding of trust and its role in our capacity to thrive. Yet strictly speaking, it is not a theory of treatment. It has no proscribed techniques or manualised therapeutic interventions. However, all relational approaches to psychotherapy are characterised by their commitment to fostering a secure attachment which the client "earns" by working alongside their therapist; the relationship *is* the therapy (Finlay, 2016). The *Relational Approach* describes a process through which a person may safely venture into their danger zone and learn to do things differently. Through a co-created relationship, the psychotherapist supports their client to develop alternatives to their outdated strategies for handling threat, along with the skills and capacity to regulate their emotional world. When we are offered a unique, attuned, non-judgemental, and authentic relationship, we are better placed to examine and explore our sense of incongruence, and seek alternative ways of responding to the world around us. This is true not just of therapeutic relationships, but for those elsewhere in our lives, which includes the realm of work.

It was Abraham Maslow who coined the term "third force" of humanism to describe the loose confederation of psychologists, philosophers, and others in the 1950s and 1960s who objected to the lop-sidedness of the then-dominant Freudian *harping on* about sickness, treatment, dread, anguish, and despair (Maslow, 1999, p. 21). Maslow along with Rogers (Person-centred) and Berne (Transactional Analysis) were far more interested in healthier processes, such as the human potential for growth and self-actualisation that lie at the heart of the humanistic therapeutic approaches. A key assumption of the humanistic approach is that our inner nature is at worst neutral or perhaps even good, and that when given the opportunity to grow we do so healthily, fruitfully, and happily. Distress arises when our authentic selves are supressed through the carelessness with which we treat each other in the relationships we encounter. Next, I focus on how attachment (especially trust) and the attitudes and values of the person-centred approach complement the practice of *Transactional Analysis*, which I discuss in more detail in Chapter 4.

Being met as a person at work. When we think of bureaucracies what we are really speaking of are oligarchies where power is concentrated in the hands of an advantaged managerial elite. Everybody who works in such an oligarchy recognises that at some level they fail the human beings who work in them. We accept this state of affairs as normal because we cannot see an alternative way to arrange ourselves. We go along with the status quo, which means working without trust, submitting to being controlled and having our intrinsic value as a person ignored. Michel's pessimistic *Iron Law* of oligarchy introduced in the previous chapter, so often used by the closed management caste to dismiss, reject, or belittle proponents of participative, democratic structures and processes, is really less of a *law* and more of a *warning* to us. We must not assume that where the exchange of money is involved, we have to cash-in our dignity (Bal, 2017). A workplace in which we can flourish is based on trust, and we can make this happen by promoting a culture of interdependency, mutual support, and collective empathy.

The *Relational Approach* I describe here is not a vision for a utopian workplace, but a way of conducting ourselves in the reality of our working lives. As a counsellor, I rely on the co-creation of a respectful relationship for therapeutic change. My work as a colleague is different, but it does not stop me from offering and expecting to receive the same quality of engagement. The *Relational Approach* I promote here emphasises that you are a human being first and a colleague second. I reject the view that you are only a means for profit, or valuable only within a narrow instrumental definition of what it is to be human. I prize your wellbeing *because* you are human, not because you can increase profit. A *Relational Approach* is most of all characterised by my imperfect striving towards being a compassionate, warm, genuine, and accepting person (Fairfield, 2013).

Researchers in attachment use the term *security priming* to acknowledge the empirical evidence supporting what psychotherapists have known for some time (Mikulincer & Shaver, 2007, 2015). That is, the effective ingredients of a secure and trusting relationship are those described by Rogers in his person-centred approach (Holmes, 1993). It is a relationship where we experience attuned responsiveness, warm acceptance, genuineness, and clear, consistent, and well-defined boundaries. The purpose of offering these conditions as a psychotherapist is to create a trusting relational ambience that can be internalised and used as an inner resource, or somewhere to go to when we feel troubled long after therapy has ended. Whilst I recognise that the workplace is not a therapeutic environment, I believe that the experience of therapy can have meaningful and perhaps even profound implications for our lives at work. I explore next the attitudes, values and processes that underpin developmentally affirming relationships that ought to be nurtured in the workplace if we are serious about flourishing.

Show me you understand. Perhaps the most poignant experience for me as a trainer is when I ask trainees to reflect on a time when they felt truly understood. For many, it brings up feelings of profound sadness. Perhaps a relative, teacher, or mentor in the past offered the experience of being understood, but on the whole, we go about our daily lives somewhat deprived of being seen for who we are. The transformative power of receiving the gift of empathy feels like an electric shock when it happens. It can be incomprehensible that somebody could put himself or herself aside for a moment, refrain from formulating a response even as you are speaking, and care enough to discover what it might be like to be you. *Empathy* means "I can sense or read your emotional states, consider them, reflect on them and then communicate what I understand about them". It reflects what a parent offers to a child when they seek reassurance or to be soothed. Attuned caregiving lets us know we are understood and not alone in the world. Without empathy, well-intentioned others who seek to help can be little more than a nuisance. Yet, a colleague who can see our problems as we see them becomes a source of inspiration. The term *mentalising* is similar to empathy, and describes the attitude of being respectful and enquiring of the mental state of another person. It goes beyond understanding feelings, and is respectful of the limits of what I can really know about you (Holmes & Slade, 2018).

At the heart of empathy is self-awareness and the ability to reflect on the active process of desiring to know both the present and changing awareness of another person. The philosopher Marcel Merleau-Ponty (1908–1961) thought in terms of: "the mystery of my relation to myself, and my own ability to adopt perspectives other than mine" (Moran, 2000, p. 432). The dance of empathy attends to the *ebb and flow* of reflecting on, then confirming the meaning of what we are hearing and sensing. The vignette in Box 3.3 deconstructs a short dialogue between Laura and Harriet. It shows the dance-like nature of the listener reflecting on what the speaker communicates, adding to what they hear and sense, and seeking verification if necessary. It requires the listener to step out of the way and allow the speaker to have all the best lines. It requires an open, unthreatened, and non-defensive attitude to ensure that feelings do not become entwined and confused, and that the listener does not metaphorically step on the speaker's toes. It requires the capacity to be calm and centred in the face of another's turmoil and distress. It is a process intimately linked with the idea of regulating the emotions of another, because only when we can ensure that our own feelings lie within manageable limits can we engage in the *dance* of empathy (Barrett-Lennard, 1981).

Box 3.3 Empathy as a dance (Steps 1→4)

1. *Speaker (Laura) becomes aware of an issue she wants to explore with her Listener (union representative Harriet). She expects, hopes, and trusts that Harriet will be receptive, and so will be vigilant about her capacity to communicate understanding.*

Laura: I wanted to talk to you about something that's really bothering me – I feel you can help because you know how things "go down" around here?

Harriet: I can see you are upset … go ahead, I will try and help.

Laura: I was passed up for promotion. I could really use the money. But am I crazy? Is it right to think it's down to the fact that I'm old and they think I'm past it? They even asked why I wanted change at this stage of my career.

2. *Listener allows the emotions to "resonate" – to become experientially alive and vivid. She communicates what she senses in the form of a tentative summary and open questions.*

Harriet: No … I don't think you're crazy. But it's not about the money is it? I wonder if it feels like you aren't being valued for what you have to offer *now*? Your wisdom … your experience. Have I got that right?

3. *Listener pauses to hear speaker's response, conveying the extent to which the Listener was accurate/helpful with their summary.*

Laura: Hmm … yeah … I had not thought of it that way. I mean, the money would be nice, but what really hurts is that being valued has a sell-by date. I have a lot to offer … why can't *now* be the right time for me to be promoted? I feel like I'm being penalised for raising my kids …

4. *Listener reflects on what is said. Satisfied that she feels the speaker understands, Laura continues with fresh content – and so the dance continues (return to stage 1).*

Harriet: And to me it feels like the company sets the timetable for being valuable, undermining those who spend time caring for others at home.

Can I be valued? *Unconditional positive regard* was a term used by Rogers to describe the fundamental attitude of deeply valuing the humanity of a person. It involves a deep regard for a person's autonomy, and their right to be self-governing. It is at the core of our socio-emotional development and thera-peutic relationships in that it helps dissolve defences raised in anticipation of being shame-worthy, unlovable, and rejected. It means caring for that person in a non-possessive way, acknowledging their right to be separate, and having permission to own their own feelings of anger, shame, and fear, for example. Psychotherapists work hard to communicate their acceptance of all that a person is, even when it is not conventionally positive or "nice". By contrast, traditional hierarchical management is rooted in a set of assumptions about human nature, most notably that people are inherently lazy, untrustworthy, and require over-sight. The fundamental tension between a *Relational Approach* and hierarchical management, then, is that it undermines the agency and wisdom of the work-force. After all, how can I communicate respect when I do not trust you?

If we swap out and invert elements of the term *unconditional positive regard*, we learn something of the attitudes that prevail in the wider world that are amplified in our organisations. *Unconditional* **negative** *regard* holds the attitude that whatever you say or do, I will dislike, dismiss, or demean you. It is the attitude that underpins sexism, racism, homophobia, and classism, for example. *Unconditional positive* **disregard** is your complete negation of me, which feels like I do not even exist. The very threat of ostracism, or "shutting somebody out", is a form of punishment in most cultures (Chapter 7). When positive regard is **conditional**, love is held hostage until certain conditions are met. For example, if we learn we are only lovable when we repress our emotions, then as adults we will struggle to express ourselves. Little boys who believe we are only lov-able if we are seen to be self-reliant and autonomous become men shamed towards extremes of self-containment, emotional inexpressiveness, toughness, and separation. Such *introjects* go some way to explain why men are less likely to seek help for their problems, and why "deaths of despair" (i.e. through sui-cide, alcohol and drug abuse) are higher amongst men compared to women in almost every culture.

How can I trust you? Authenticity is at the heart of how we learn to trust others. Can I trust *you* to recognise and admit when you are unfair or in the wrong? Can I trust *you* to know when to say sorry, and begin the healing when trust is undermined? Trusting another to recognise when they are behaving unfairly or inconsistently is at the very heart of feeling secure with another person – or an organisation for that matter. Authenticity requires an awareness of the flow of feelings and sensations as we work with others. It requires a willingness to communicate this awareness in an appropriate and timely way. Barriers to being authentic include wanting to be right, wanting to be admired, or failing to acknowledge difficult emotions such as the big three of fear, anger, or shame. This brings us back to the notion of affect (emotional) regulation: "can I survive my emotions if things get difficult?"

The reflective exercise in Box 3.4 invites you to consider how authentic you are in expressing your emotions. Does it feel safe to show how you feel at work? Is it possible your emotional world is downregulated in your workplace relationships? There is no right or wrong answer here because there are many reasons why it may feel unsafe to bring your whole self to the workplace. We spend more time reflecting on our identities in the workplace in the final chapter.

Box 3.4 Reflections on authenticity

Consider how you usually express your feelings in words, and/or non-verbally:

- When you are feeling bored with what is going on around you.
- When you feel annoyed with someone you want to build a better relationship with.
- When another person says or does something that hurts your feelings.
- When you feel emotionally overwhelmed by what someone else has said.
- When you feel competitive.
- When you feel excluded from what is going on.

Now consider the different ways you have of expressing yourself in these situations. What "rules" have you learnt about how you express yourself? How much emotional labour or *acting* do you do in these situations (see Chapter 1)? Would it be useful to change any of the ways you have of expressing your feelings in a more congruent and authentic way? What stops you from doing this?

Tolerating the cycle of disruption and repair. Conflict and tension between colleagues is inevitable from time to time, and perhaps even necessary to remind us we are real, authentic human beings. The seasoned psychotherapist, the reflective and well-resourced carer, or the most saintly and considerate colleague need only aspire to being what the psychoanalyst Donald Winnicott termed "good enough" when attempting to consistently offer a *Relational Approach* to others. I for one cannot possibly meet the demands of the organisation, or my colleagues, all of the time. There will be times when I let them down, miss deadlines, make mistakes, disagree, or simply upset people by not complying with their sometimes unspoken expectations. It is all too human to feel distracted, avoidant, anxious, or chaotic when called on to attend to the needs of others in a consistent and attuned way. At these times, we can be met with blame, hurt, anger, and disappointment when in fact what we really need is a moment to reflect.

A *Relational Approach* understands that we need not necessarily avoid conflict with colleagues. It does not have to be the end of the world. The so-called "disruption–repair" cycle lies at the heart of feeling emotionally secure, self-confident, and mature in our relationships (Schore, 2003). When we feel secure in our working relationships, we understand that we will not be left in distress for too long if things go wrong. Indeed, by understanding that conflict is *not* the end of the world, we can foster confidence in our capacity to engage in enduring, robust, and perhaps even fulfilling relationships. Colleagues who stay sufficiently open to the experience of conflict, and resist the temptation to blame whilst enduring the discomfort of strong emotions, are more likely to arrive at a satisfying resolution. In the act of resolution we foster deeper levels of trust with each other, which in turn helps us understand that our relationships are a place where we can feel secure enough to be accepted for who we really are, warts and all. The next section considers the blame game, or how we think about blame, its influence on the way we handle conflict, and how it can be linked with our relational security.

The blame game. The psychiatrist Eric Berne (1910–1970) developed his theory of communication as he had become impatient with the inaccessibility and slowness of the practice of psychotherapy as he saw it at the time. A keen observer of people and having reflected on three painful divorces, he developed an unpretentious language to describe the practice of relationships. The Transactional Analysis (TA) framework is popular especially in organisational settings because it offers a no-nonsense language to describe and then a vantage point from which to modify our relationships (Mountain & Davidson, 2011). Long before the development of attachment theory, Berne saw how the convictions we adopt about ourselves (i.e. I matter, *or* I do not matter), and others (You matter *or* You do not matter) shape whether relationships helped us feel either great or lousy. The problem as he saw it was that once our convictions take shape in childhood, we use them without question (i.e. introjects) as the lens through which to *do* relationships. He was rightfully optimistic that, with a little self-awareness, we could rewrite our evaluations and learn to relate in ways that are more authentic and helpful. We can map the ideas around trust that lie at the heart of attachment theory with the practical skills of TA by thinking about *blame* in terms of anger directed either at ourselves or others. When under stress we can default to habitually unhelpful evaluations of others and ourselves through the *blame game*. This is a straightforward framework for raising self-awareness and increasing our menu of relationship options (Box 3.5).

Box 3.5 The blame game

When I blame:	My outlook is:	Attachment strategy
You	*positive* about me, but *negative* about you	Avoidant
Me	*negative* about me, but *positive* about you	Anxious
Everyone	*negative* about me, and *negative* about you	Fearful
Nobody	*positive* about me, and *positive* about you	Secure

It is an approach amenable also to the metaphor of a compass, which guides us through the landscape of both attachment *thinking* and TA *practice* (Griffin & Bartholomew, 1994; see Figure 3.2). When under stress or pressure – in a rush with a deadline, or just tired – it can be easy to lose our trust in others and ourselves and stray from the security of the NW point of the compass. It can be immensely empowering to understand how the assumptions I make about trust in you or me colour my style of relating. Consider the three scenarios in Box 3.6 and ask how you might widen your menu of choices and navigate a way back to a more empowered *North-West* or secure perspective.

Figure 3.2 The way my evaluations link TA with attachment strategies.

Box 3.6 Navigating the landscape of trust

- *She makes such a mess of things – I wish she would just ask my advice before going ahead and creating chaos.* Here, the assumption is that I need to do things for you because I do not believe you have the capacity to do things for yourself. This is a positive *me* and negative *you* position and right now I am firmly in avoidant *South-West* territory. It is likely I will not even ask whether you actually want my help. This perspective edges towards the kind of micromanagement consistent with emotional abuse (Chapter 7).
- *I can't do this technical stuff – I'll just leave the photocopier jammed for someone else to sort out.* Here, I adopt the position where I believe I am less competent than you: this negative *me* but positive *you* position lies in the anxious *North-East*. It just feels too risky to act like a "grown-up" because I imagine everyone is more able and competent than me.
- *I have no idea how to make this damn computer work – and there is no point calling the idiots in IT for help.* This is an apparently hopeless negative *me* and negative *you* *South-East* fearful orientation. Because everybody is to blame, I become stuck in a place of powerlessness.

Things to keep in mind

- The big three fundamental emotions of anger, fear, and shame lie beneath the surface of our relationships, shaping how we minimise danger in our environment.
- Attachment is a way to understand our dynamic, co-created relationship with trust. Our strategies are not immutable and fixed, but are plastic and open to change and renegotiation.
- Attachment is not a theory of practice, but it does inform a humanistic *Relational Approach* which has at its core accurate and attuned empathy, warm acceptance, and authenticity.
- It is not all plain sailing. The capacity to tolerate the cycle of disruption and repair forms the basis of trust, and contributes to robustness in a democratic workplace where we can all flourish.

References

Bal M. (2017). *Dignity in the workplace: New theoretical perspectives.* Basingstoke: Palgrave Macmillan.

Barrett-Lennard GT. (1981). The empathy cycle. *Journal of Counselling Psychology,* 28(2), 91–100.

Byrne Z, Albert L, Manning S, & Desir R. (2017). Relational models and engagement: An attachment theory perspective. *Journal of Managerial Psychology,* 32(1), 30–44.

Crittenden PM. (2012). *The development of protective attachment strategies across the lifespan.* Lecture: British Psychological Society Annual Conference. Available from: www.youtube.com/watch?v=XvK35ocdytw [Accessed 20.12.18].

Ein-Dor T & Hirschberger G. (2016). Rethinking attachment theory: from a theory of relationships to a theory of individual and group survival. *Current Directions in Psychological Science,* 25(4), 223–227.

Fairfield M. (2013). The relational movement. *British Gestalt Journal,* 22(1), 22–35.

Finlay L. (2016). *Relational integrative psychotherapy.* Chichester: Wiley Blackwell.

Gilbert P & Andrews B. (1998). *Shame: Interpersonal behaviour, psychopathology and culture.* Oxford: Oxford University Press.

Griffin D & Bartholomew K. (1994). Models of the self and other: Fundamental dimensions underlying measures of adult attachment. *Journal of Personality and Social Psychology,* 67(3), 430–445.

Harms PD. (2011). Adult attachment styles in the workplace. *Human Resource Management Review,* 21, 285–296.

Holmes J. (1993). *John Bowlby & attachment theory.* London: Routledge.

Holmes J & Slade A. (2018). *Attachment in therapeutic practice.* London: Sage.

Landa S & Duschinsky R. (2013). Crittenden's dynamic-maturational model of attachment and adaptation. *Review of General Psychology,* 17(3), 326–338.

Maslow AH. (1999). *Toward a psychology of being* (3rd ed.). New York: John Wiley & Sons.

Mikulincer M & Shaver PR. (2007). Boosting attachment security to promote mental health, prosocial values, and inter-group tolerance. *Psychological Inquiry,* 18(3), 139–156.

Mikulincer M & Shaver PR. (2015). The psychological effects of the contextual activation of security-enhancing mental representations in adulthood. *Current Opinion in Psychology,* 1, 18–21.

Moran D. (2000). *Introduction to phenomenology.* London: Routledge.

Mountain A & Davidson C. (2011). *Working together: Organizational transactional analysis and business performance.* Aldershot: Gower Publishing.

Pavuluri MN, Henry D, & Allen K. (2002). Anxiety and fear: Discriminant validity in the child and adolescent practitioner's perspective. *European Child & Adolescent Psychiatry,* 11, 273–280.

Schore A. (2003). *Affect dysregulation and disorders of the self.* New York: W.W. Norton & Co.

Scrima F, Di Stefano G, Guarnaccia C, & Lorito L. (2015). The impact of adult attachment style on organizational commitment and adult attachment in the workplace. *Personality and Individual Differences,* 86, 432–437.

Yip J, Ehrhardt K, Black H, & Walker DO. (2018). Attachment theory at work: A review and directions for future research. *Journal of Organizational Behavior,* 39, 185–198.

Chapter 4

The crowded workplace

Adults, children, and parents

I have a black and white postcard pinned to the wall above my desk showing rows and rows of workers sat in front of their computers viewed from the rear of the room with the caption: "If you liked school – you'll *LOVE* work". The similarity between the workplace and experiences from our childhood goes beyond the superficial. Although your colleagues appear to be adults, we are all in fact buffeted by a riotous crowd of the children within us all, doing the things kids like to do such as play, bully, and get up to mischief. Attempting to reign in this unruly lot are the metaphorical parents, teachers, and other authority figures from our past who come together creating our own, completely unique work-based family system or organogram.

Colleagues will remind you, perhaps out of awareness, of family members, key figures from your past, and maybe even a much-maligned pet. Unwittingly, we are drawn into relationship dynamics from the past that often do not fit the present. If you do not believe me, try listening out for the evidence around you: "I'm *so* disappointed … I expected more from you"; "OK settle down everyone … let's get back to work"; "Give that job to Jack … he's always willing to please"; "He needs to *grow up* and get on with it"; "She's so *serious* … no fun at all"; "I love starting new projects … I get bored so easily"; "*Wow* … that's completely amazing …"; "She's sooo bossy … like having a big sister" (see also Box 4.1).

Eric Berne, introduced in the previous chapter, was a keen observer of people both in and outside his consulting room. He noticed how we seem to shift around between readily observable and fairly consistent types of behaviours. Our gestures, attitudes, and ways of talking all seemed to correlate with sets of emotions and ways of thinking. It appeared obvious to him that these relational *states* reflect the fact that we were all *children*, were dependent on some *parental* figure, and learnt to develop grown-up or *adult* relating skills through teachers, for example. In other words, our internalised metaphorical states reflect how we communicate our emotions (the *Child*), inherited values and rules (the

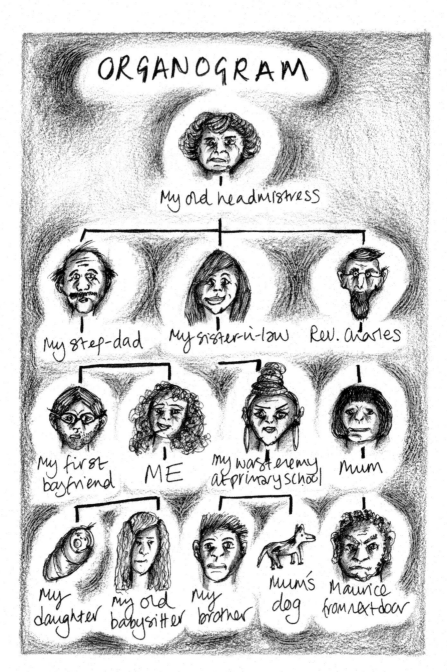

Figure 4.1 Organogram.

Parent), and how we balance them both through being reasonable and rational (the *Adult*). We capitalise the initials of these terms to distinguish our metaphorical *ego states* from their meaning in the wider world.

Some criticise Berne's model because of its apparent rigidity and oversimplification of our emotional substructures. Navigating the varied and often contradictory social settings that we encounter at work requires we adopt an equally sophisticated array of selves or configurations, as discussed earlier in Chapter 2. Nevertheless, the idea of *Parent, Child*, and *Adult* ego states, which I discuss next, are compellingly useful handles for reflecting on how our observable interpersonal relationship styles and inner worlds are shaped, fashioned, and informed by the past. Besides, the model gives us a really useful vantage point from which to examine exactly who is "behind the steering wheel" at any given time.

Box 4.1 Reflective Exercise 1. *Adults, parents, and children at work*

When thinking about work, are you reminded of:

- Any critical messages from your childhood?
- Protective, sympathetic, or nurturing messages?
- A colleague who seems to accept more work than they should?
- Someone with a particularly short fuse?
- A person who is quick to find faults with others?
- Anyone at work who is enthusiastic, playful, or spontaneous?

Do any of the final four of the above remind you of yourself?

The *Parent* ego state is like the judicial system of our inner world, and he or she is shaped by the values and attitudes of our own unique experience of being cared for. When I notice that I am adopting certain postures or gestures – such as when my hands go to my hips, my finger feels drawn to wagging, or when I have the urge to "tell" someone what they ought to do – I have drifted into a stereotypical *Parent* mode. The *Parent* is a coin with *both* Nurturing and Critical sides.

The *Nurturing* Parent cares, praises, and comforts, offering compassion, understanding, and warmth when they suspect it is needed. As kids we practiced care and compassion (e.g. taking care of a baby brother, nurturing a doll, hosting imaginary tea parties), because our carers modelled this behaviour. Nurturing implies a positive regard for those we seek to support, and there are many ways we show this at work, such as when offering help: "just let me know if you need a hand". The negative counterpart of nurturing would be to take over another persons project and do it for them. Although we appear to be nurturing, the message we send is: "I don't think you are good enough". The commonly encountered sexist terms "smother mother" or "mother hen" are often used to describe a type of behaviour which, although well-meaning, does in fact undermine and infantilise the person being micromanaged.

The *Critical* Parent is blaming, prejudiced, and judgemental, both of themselves and others. It is most obvious when we interrupt others, are defensive when presented with feedback, or pull rank when feeling threatened. We may experience the *Critical* ego state when preparing to make a presentation to our peers, for example. In believing that we won't be taken seriously, we hear the voice of a parent or teacher who may have said: "you are not up to it". This message is often experienced as an automatic response when we feel anxious, and because it is so deeply ingrained it may be difficult to identify at first. However, when the metaphor of an ego state is understood, we can begin to simply notice and not beat ourselves up about the fact that we may have drifted into *Critical Parent* mode, identifiable through the rolling of eyes, crossing of arms, wagging of fingers, etc.

The *Child* is the earliest ego state to develop, and incorporates child-like behaviours and emotions unique to our own relationship history. When inhabiting the Child ego state, I think, feel, and behave in the ways I did when I was younger. The Child can be responsible for startling creativity and impulsiveness, and like the Adult is a coin with two sides.

The *Adapted* Child is strongly influenced – both positively and negatively – by the behaviour of our early carers. As grown-ups we are compelled to spend a lot of our time in this state as there are just so many rules and conventions to which we feel we must unquestioningly adhere (Chapter 2). We adapt our ways of behaving based on our childhood patterns when we feel they may not be appropriate to grown-up situations. For example, I may want to speak up and say "but the king has no clothes", but do not because I fear rocking the boat. We defer to authority figures, thinking and acting in anticipation of what a manager or peers might think of us. This leads to assumptions about there being something "wrong" with me that must change to be acceptable, to fit in, or be approved of. For some who adapt to parental messages about how "bad" it is to express anger, for example, adulthood may mean the repression, redirection, or projection of that anger in ways that require some heavy-duty emotional labour or self-soothing, say, through alcohol, food, shopping, workaholism, and so on. The belief that, like "Eeyore", the pessimistic donkey from *Winnie the Pooh*, "nothing has ever gone right for me in the past, so no matter what I do, nothing will go right for me in the future" becomes a self-fulfilling myth (Adams, 2009).

As the first-born of my siblings, I simply learnt to expect that I would be treated differently to others, because the rules that applied to my brothers did not apply to me. On Friday evenings, for instance, when they were already in bed, I was allowed to watch TV and eat fish and chips with the grown-ups. My

Adapted Child merely conformed to the expectations of his parents, which was that the rules did not apply to me. This might go some way to explaining my ambivalent (to say the least) attitude towards authority or being told what to do. I wonder if it is time to give some thought to how your early experiences with siblings, assuming you have them, or carers, shaped your Adapted Child? What are your attitudes to authority, entitlement, and responsibility, for example? Are they helpful to you in your current context?

The *Free* Child ego state, on the other hand, is pleasure-seeking, impulsive, and expressive – free of the rules and limits imposed by parental or authority figures. We like to play, explore, tell stories and jokes, and are always curious about trying new stuff and working visually to understand and explain things. At times, our Free Child can seem like the most engaging and charming of the ego states, although he or she is also capable of doing whatever is necessary to get what they want. Temper tantrums, rebellion, and bullying can be a characteristic of this part of ourselves (Chapter 7). In Free Child mode, every situation is an opportunity, and we like to take advantage of all of them, often acting before we think. It is the part of ourselves that adopts a "*Positive self – Positive other*" life position; no real need for power games because everyone counts.

I was lucky enough to grow up in an environment that was boisterous, spontaneous, and playful. Halloween, for example, was a riot of apple bobbing, treacle, and water fights that involved the grown-ups too. Emotions – both positive and negative – were allowed to flow and could be expressed safely. For me, play did not bring with it the fear that things might run out of control and become frightening, but as a grown-up I learnt that this was not everybody's experience of play. Indeed, the greatest challenge on becoming a parent can be the constant invitation to engage in carefree play with kids. Not all of us are lucky enough to learn how to play when we were young. What might be fun for me may not be fun for you, so trust must first be built before we can be sure that playful teasing, for example, won't hurt others.

The *Adult* ego state is a metaphor for the analytical, rational thinking part of me, and is sometimes seen as being like the *computer* inside. We are all capable of processing information from the world, but unlike other ego states, the Adult is clearly anchored in the *present* and uncontaminated by the past. The Adult can in principle understand both the *pros* and *cons* of a given situation from a relatively objective perspective. The Adult differs from the Parent in being *authoritative* as opposed to *authoritarian*. In addition to being the negotiator between Parent and Child ego states, my Adult also proposes alternatives to the gut feelings that can draw me into acting in response to some given experience or situation. It is a bit like having an internalised mentor or supervisor (as discussed in Chapter 5). Consider the exercise in Box 4.2 (my suggested answers are at the end of chapter), and try to identify which ego state a response may come from. Do any feel familiar to you from the context of your work?

Box 4.2 Identify your Adult, Parent, and Child responses in the following situations

1.   *You arrive at the printer and see it isn't working.*
   (i)   "I'll do a quick check to see if it's something obvious, otherwise I'll contact Lisa and ask her to fix it this morning."
   (ii)   "What a pain in the neck – I'd like to kick the damn thing to bits."
   (iii)   "I bet it's John's fault – he's *always* leaving me to sort out his problems."

2.   *Gerry, who is new to the team, loses some important notes. His manager says:*
   (i)   "I told you to keep track of notes … just sort it out … it's your responsibility."
   (ii)   "Check with everybody who's been in the office this morning … I expect they were picked up in error …"
   (iii)   "Don't look at me … I didn't take them …"

3.   *Harveen, who has been in the department for less time than you, gets promoted.*
   (i)   "I'll show them … I'll hold back on that report, then they'll know how valuable I am around here."
   (ii)   "I thought I would be the stronger candidate, but it seems I've got some blind spots – I'll talk to my manager for some feedback."
   (iii)   "But I'm more qualified than her … they just need more women in those positions because it looks better!"

4.   *Izabella loses her temper with a new member of the team. Her manager thinks:*
   (i)   "She's such a hot-head … doesn't surprise me … time to throw the book at her … she's a bully."
   (ii)   "I need to hear her side of the story … there is obviously something going on; it can't be allowed to disrupt the team."
   (iii)   "Ugh … I didn't sign up for this … I'll just let them sort themselves out."

5.   *Toby misses a deadline, tearfully explaining that his relationship is in difficulty.*
   (i)   "Let's go somewhere quiet, and you can tell me *all* about it …"
   (ii)   "I think it's unprofessional to bring your romantic difficulties into the workplace … pull yourself together."
   (iii)   "Tell me what deadlines you have coming up and we'll get them off your desk until you feel better able to manage …"

Clues to your ego states. In Table 4.1 I have collected a fairly standard matrix of words, tones of voice, gestures, and expressions that are clues to someone's current ego state (see Villeré, 1981). The idea that you can use them as a diagnostic tool for identifying Child-, Adult-, and Parent-like behaviours is to misunderstand the power of the metaphor. When I inhabit *my* Free Child, for example, it will be associated with my own unique childhood experiences. This is not to say that Table 4.1 is irrelevant. It is an invitation to reflect more deeply on how you are in relationships.

Using your laptop or a large sheet of paper, create a blank version of Table 4.1. Begin populating it with your own personal clues about how you are at work. Thinking about context can also help. How are you with authority figures, colleagues who you find it easy to be with, and those who you would prefer to avoid? Is there something about them that draws you in or pushes you away? Do they remind you of people from your past? Is there something about them that perhaps reminds you of yourself? Think about the tasks you enjoy doing and those that you really dislike. How do you feel or respond to them? And what about people you work with who you really admire. Is there anyone you try to emulate? Stick to what people might be able to observe or hear when they are around you, rather than what they might have to try and imagine about you. If you have trusted colleagues, perhaps ask them to give you feedback as you create your own *Table of Clues*. I will say something about blind spots next, but you might find the *Triad Method* (Box 4.3) a useful tool not only for this exercise, but for developing your *Relational Approach* more generally.

Blind spots come about because of the gap that exists between self-perceptions and how others see us. We all see ourselves in ways that are not necessarily shared by others. In fact, it is increasingly acknowledged that a person's accurate perception of themselves is relatively limited. The socialite and amateur soprano Florence Foster Jenkins (1868–1944), who had a lifelong passion for performance, was infamous for her blind spot (or should it be deaf spot?) for how "exquisitely bad" she was, even in the estimation of her most ardent fans. Irrespective of why, and in the case of Jenkins it is thought neurosyphilis played its part, none of us can really hope to hear ourselves as others do. Others are better placed to offer us valid and sometimes uncomfortable-to-acknowledge information about how we come across, either because we are unable or unwilling to look in the mirror and see ourselves as others do (Gallrein et al., 2013).

All relationships are potential opportunities to exchange information and engage in a dynamic process that can help us develop self-awareness through feedback and disclosure. Of course, it is important to carefully choose who we seek feedback from. We should bear in mind that when we provide a close acquaintance with feedback, we are necessarily providing an evaluation of someone we presumably choose to spend time with. To receive feedback about how others see us, we need simply be *curious* about our thoughts, feelings,

Table 4.1 Generic clues to ego states

	Child		Adult	Parent	
	Adapted	Free		Nurturing	Critical
I'm interested in …	me		things	you	
Words often used	Can't, won't	Wow!, Hi, cool, fun	Correct, how?, what?, why?	Good, excellent, concerned	Bad, should, ought, must
The tone of voice	Whiney Defiant Demanding	Loud Energetic Enthusiastic	Even Precise Monotone	Saccharine Comforting Loving	Critical Firm Dismissing
Gestures and expressions	Pouting Sad	Loose Uninhibited	Thoughtful Alert	Accepting Smiling	Frowning Pointy fingers
Posture	Closed Uptight	Relaxed Agile	Upright	Leaning in	Shoulders up Hands on hips
Attitude	Compliant Demanding Submissive	Curious Fun-loving Spontaneous	Interested Observant Evaluative	Understanding Caring Giving	Authoritarian Moralistic Judgemental

intuitions, attitudes, assumptions, and beliefs. The process of increasing self-knowledge never ceases, and our ability to understand and perhaps be helpful to others is limited by the extent to which we are willing to know ourselves.

Joseph Luft and Harrington Ingham (1955) pioneered a systematic approach to analysing the relationship between self-perceptions and how others see us through their four-way Johari grid. Originally visualised as a rigid window frame, I prefer to see it instead as a dynamic relational tool; a series of interconnected rooms linked by passageways and doors, hidden from myself and others, in which aspects of who I am (i.e. configurations of self), known and unknown, can be explored. It is not a static architecture, but a dynamic, shifting environment, expanding and contracting depending on who I am with and the social groupings I belong to. While exploring the rooms can lead to greater self-awareness, it is also important to recognise that the floorplan of our configurations can never be entirely known or mapped out (Figure 4.2).

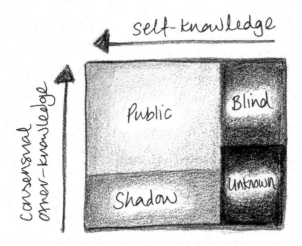

Figure 4.2 Johari rooms.

- *The Public Area.* This is where I share what is known equally to me and to you. Obvious information appears here such as my physical characteristics and differences, as well as other things I want you to know about me, which includes feelings. Consistent with the idea of congruence, our life's goal is to ensure that this is the largest room. *I can do this through self-disclosure and developing self-awareness.*
- *The Blind Area.* This is what everybody else thinks about me, but I either cannot or do not wish to see. It could, for example, include my mannerisms,

body language, and other aspects of my behaviour. Others use this information to draw conclusions about me and my attitudes. The adjectives used in this area are those chosen by others to describe me. Perhaps I am seen as calm and confident, when in fact I feel very different inside. *There is always something to be learned by asking others what they think of us, and this practice will decrease the size of this space.*

- *The Shadow Area.* The hidden self may include secrets, experiences, or fears that I feel ashamed about sharing. The adjectives used in this room are chosen by me alone; I do not share them readily. *The shadows can be reduced by disclosing more about my hidden self to those I trust – moving what is hidden about me out of the shadows* (see Chapter 7).

- *Unknown Area.* This is the part of me that is out of awareness – to everybody. It represents my motivations, unconscious needs, anxieties, or undiscovered potential. Putting myself in new situations outside my comfort zone reveals more of my unknown self, but being gloriously human means that there will always be unknowns. *Engaging reflectively in relationships – which can include counselling – reduces this area by gradually accessing memories, and developing insight.*

Introducing *Transactions*

The construct of ego states is a useful approach for understanding our processes of communication, and TA is well known for its visual representations of how we engage with each other (Stewart & Joines, 2012). The familiar trio of stacked rings that represent the metaphorical Child, Adult, and Parent (CAP) ego states are shown in Figure 4.3. For now, we assess which ego state we inhabit just on the basis of observable behaviours, and we will take a closer look at what might lie behind them in the next section. If a person is clear and coherent in the way they are talking, are standing upright and engaging in eye contact, and they convey some sense of flexibility in the way they see a situation, then they are in all likelihood inhabiting their Adult ego state. If you were in a conversation with somebody in this ego state, there is a strong invitation to reciprocate:

Karen (A1): I've noticed that it's sometimes difficult for you to make it to our early meetings. I was wondering whether we could find a solution because I value what we achieve together.

Mark (A2): Oh … er … thanks … (*surprised*). I appreciate that. Well … I do struggle getting here at that time because I have to drop my youngest off at nursery. Could we meet at nine instead? Is that OK?

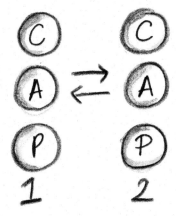

Figure 4.3 An example of an *Adult* to *Adult* parallel transaction (i.e. A1 ↔ A2).

This is an example of a *parallel transaction* because the ego state addressed is the one that responds (i.e. Figure 4.3, A1 ↔ A2). It is a dialogue that could proceed indefinitely in a positive way, but not all parallel transactions are just so. However, what is important to notice is that both Karen and Mark are working from a *"positive self and positive other"* position, otherwise referred to as an *Adult* to *Adult* transaction. These kinds of transactions ensure the co-creation of a working space where much more could happen if it was necessary, because an invitation extended to someone's Adult ego state is more likely to be taken up, or *hooked*. So long as both Karen and Mark are interested in *hooking* into one another's Adult ego state, the conversation will continue to some logical, mutually satisfying conclusion.

Consider the following conversation involving an exasperated Kelly and her more anxious colleague, Peter:

Kelly (P1): You are an experienced scientist yet you seem to have ignored all our Health and Safety risk assessments, endangering the wellbeing of everyone in the lab.

Peter (C2): Well … if it wasn't for the fact that I'm so bloody tired and overworked because you give me so many unrealistic deadlines then maybe I would have been able to do my job properly.

Kelly (P1): What a shame you have taken this attitude Peter … I'm *really* disappointed in you.

As Kelly begins the transaction, Peter, on reflection, might have recognised that he was re-experiencing being about 12 years old when scolded by a teacher (i.e. P1 → C2). In the *here and now*, he received a compelling invitation by Kelly to respond from his Child ego state (i.e. C2 → P1). Perhaps being unaware of this strong invitation or *hook*, Peter allowed his 12-year-old self to metaphorically take control and jump into the driving seat. Feeling threatened and under attack, he responds defensively, i.e. he was working from a *"negative self, negative other"* position. This invited the corresponding punitive parental response from Kelly, leading to a drama reminiscent of playgrounds and boardrooms alike. But, let's not focus solely on Peter here, because Kelly initiated the exchange from a position of *"positive self, negative other"* through her punitive and blaming opening *hook* aimed at Peter's Child ego state. So here is another example of a *parallel transaction* because it could go on indefinitely. Kelly becomes exacerbated with Peter's defensiveness and Peter feels increasingly attacked and blamed, so becomes defensive (i.e. P1 ↔ C2). Other *parallel* transactions include Child–Child and Parent–Parent. Now reflect on a recent encounter that left you feeling dissatisfied or upset. Is it possible that it involved this type of exchange? Do you recall an opening *hook* that triggered you? Could the blame game help you navigate your way to a more satisfying resolution (see Chapter 3)?

Surprises in our transactions. After an initial and cooperative *parallel* exchange between Stan and Jane (i.e. A1 → A2), Stan attempts a disruptive *crossed* Child *hook* (C1) in an attempt to engage either Jane's Child (C1 → C2) or Parent (C1 → P2) ego states.

Stan (A1): So the taxi to the station is picking us up from the office at 8 am … is there anything you would like me to bring along?
Jane (A2): Oh yes, don't forget the Stress Risk Assessments for the Department, we could use the time to review them on the train.
Stan (C1): Couldn't we just get slightly sloshed on expenses instead? Health and Safety is sooo boring …

A parallel response from Jane (i.e. C2 below) would undoubtedly lead to a chaotic, and perhaps more entertaining trip. Alternatively, the more punitive critical Parent response (i.e. P2) would certainly put Stan in his place, and perhaps shame him from a Free to Adaptive Child position. This is a favourite tactic of those who get a kick out of telling people off or putting others in their place. But because we can choose to transact in whatever way we want, Jane wisely acknowledges the playfulness of Stan's *hook*, yet remains nevertheless in Adult mode as she invites him back into a parallel style of Adult relating (i.e. A2).

Jane (C2): I know … dull as ditch water … let's do that … it'll be such a laugh …

Jane (P2): I'm disappointed in you Stan … that's quite an immature attitude …

Jane (A2): That's a fun idea … but think of the risk assessment we would have to write (laughs) … lets stick to cappuccinos?

So, when transactions are crossed in this way (i.e. Stan = C1), there is a strong invitation for the other person to switch their ego states. The crossing of ego states is often accompanied by feelings of surprise, a mild jolt, or in the extreme, a flash of anger (for examples see *Breaking Transaction Patterns* Box 4.4). The person initiating the crossed transaction may not be consciously aware that they are doing this, but again, *we do have choices about how we respond.* From Stan's perspective, perhaps a female manager reminds him – out of conscious awareness – of a disapproving school teacher, and so the prospect of spending time with a powerful female figure creates sufficient stress for him to zoom back to ways of coping from his childhood (see the next section where we discuss *transference*). Perhaps deflecting a teacher's disapproval by goofing around was a behaviour Stan learnt to manage his anxiety? There are two factors which tend to make it more likely that we will be *hooked* to childhood scripts in this way (Stewart & Joines, 2012, chapter 11):

- When the *here and now* situation is perceived as stressful.
- When we perceive some resemblance between the *here and now* situation and a situation in childhood we experienced as stressful.

What is useful about TA is that it is a tried and tested tool for decoupling the powerful *rubber bands* that zip us back to childhood scripts of behaviour (i.e. attachment strategies, Chapter 3). When we are in so-called script mode, we are attempting to address adult challenges by replaying strategies learnt in childhood. With Adult awareness, Stan can begin to recognise that people in the here and now – such as Jane – are very different from unpleasant or scary teachers from the past.

Counsellors and psychotherapists spend years in their own therapy discovering their own *drivers, hooks,* and so on, to better understand when and how our childhood scripts are being triggered, which would be problematic in a therapeutic setting. Again, I fully recognise that the workplace is not a therapeutic environment, but developing an awareness of our more obvious hooks and drivers will ensure that our encounters are more satisfying and productive.

The Triad Method is perhaps the most powerful tool for developing self-awareness when working with Transactions (Box 4.3). It can be used to re-enact Transactions such as those above, and for experimenting with new ways of *Breaking Transaction Patterns* (see Box 4.4). When attempting these exercises, focus on staying within your Adult ego state, or perhaps try mixing it up with the Nurturing Parent/Free Child states. Notice how inhabiting our Adult state makes it much easier to observe what I call the *Rogerian rule*, namely (Kirschenbaum, 2007, p. 318):

> *Each person speaks up only after they have first restated the ideas and feelings of the previous speaker accurately, and to their satisfaction.*

Box 4.3 The triad method

The triad method was created to develop communication skills and self-awareness (Spice & Spice, 1976). It generally involves groups of three (*triads*) turn-taking in an activity with each other. Reflective learning is facilitated by feedback from the perspectives of those taking the roles of *listener*, *speaker*, and *observer*, respectively. By sharing the experience of applying skills (*listener*), observing others (*observer*), and experiencing different listening styles (*speaker*), participants create a situation where they can appreciate an encounter from all perspectives. The silent *observer* in particular offers a unique insight detached from *in the moment* active listening, along with a record of what has occurred between the *speaker* and the *listener*.

Feedback helps us become more aware of what we do and how we do it. Receiving feedback gives us an opportunity to change and modify our behaviour and to become more effective in our encounters. To be helpful, feedback happens in the sequence L → S → O. The *Listener* first describes their experience, the *Speaker* then follows, and finally the *Observer* feeds back to *Speaker*. Feedback needs to be offered in a concerned and supportive way, focusing on:

- respecting and recognising both strengths and areas for development
- behaviours rather than the person
- observations rather than inferences
- descriptions rather than judgements
- being specific rather than generalising
- sharing ideas and information rather than giving advice
- information the receiver can use, rather than what we would like to say
- behaviours the speaker can actually change.

Box 4.4 Breaking transaction patterns

Identify the ego states in the exchanges between A and B below. Can you formulate an ADULT response which might invite a break in the pattern of relating? You could role play solutions using *The Triad Method*.

For example

A "I want these reports ready by Monday morning. Could you look at them over the weekend"?

B "Sorry Bob ... your bad planning is not my emergency."

Alternatively

B "I won't have time to do this over the weekend, but it is possible to get it done before I leave the office today if you help me re-prioritise my other commitments for next week."

A "So ... (*glancing at watch*) if you could conclude your point Tony ... I'm aware others would like to contribute ... and we have a lot to cover today ..."

B "How dare you treat me like this ... you're not even interested in what I have to say" (*gesturing to his own wrist*).

A "I apologise if that's how it seemed ... I was just checking for time ... it's my role as Chair of the meeting to ..."

B "This is typical of the way management dismisses the concerns of staff ..."

A "Look Tony (*angrily*) ... if you continue to behave this way I'll throw you out of the meeting ..."

A "You're late again? Is this *really* consistent with someone who wants to be promoted?"

B "I'm really sorry ... I'll try not to do it again."

A "But it's becoming a habit ... isn't it?"

B "Look I've said I'm sorry ... I can't help it if ... (defensively)"

A "This is such a boring task ... I hate doing it (*with a yawn*) ... so, what did you get up to at the weekend?"

B "Yeah ... these reports never get read anyway ... I thought I would get a tattoo ... want to see it?"

Tangential and Blocked Transactions. Conversations in the workplace are some-times intended, perhaps unconsciously, to deflect, defend, or block someone from engaging in an authentic or congruent manner. Let me illustrate this using the example of Norman, who seeks to deflect Sally's invitation to have a conversation. He suspects, correctly, that she is concerned he may be avoiding team meetings:

Sally (1): Hi Norm, haven't seen you at team meetings for a while … how are you doing?

Norman (1): Sorry … must dash … er … very busy … lots to do … (*backing away*)

Sally (2): Oh … er ….Yes … I'm really up to my neck too … Look … it seems this type of thing isn't a priority for you right now … Have I got that right?

Blocking and deflecting are especially common tactics if the conversation is potentially stressful, difficult, or poses a challenge to the person you are trying to engage. In the example above, Sally seems initially to have taken Norman's bait of a *tangential* response, and he even begins his strategic withdrawal. However, by sticking to her original objective, Sally brings the conversation back to pursuing what may be getting in the way of Norman's engagement. Other defensive strategies for blocking or keeping people at arm's length include: *prevarication* (e.g. splitting hairs, more said in Chapter 7), *intellectualising* (e.g. moving into a detached, heady type of discussion), or *blathering* (e.g. filling the space with long and irrelevant stories that are in fact silencing and designed to keep you at a distance).

In a therapeutic environment, counsellors spend a lot of time working with defences which, for a variety of reasons, are behaviours intended to keep others emotionally apart. In the therapeutic context it is important to recog-nise that defences perform an important function, and here it is powerful to acknowledge them without judgement, even recognising their usefulness in keeping us safe in a dangerous world. It would be congruent to communicate my own responses and reactions to someone's defences by saying something like: "when you intellectualise I feel pushed away", for example. And like the workplace, blocking transactions are a tactic used to avoid addressing issues that threaten or undermine the frame of reference of someone. Noticing that we are being blocked should alert us to being respectful of *why* a person might be doing this, because at some level, they feel endangered or threatened.

Box 4.5 Reflective Exercise 2. *Working with defences*

This exercise works best using the *Triad Method*. The purpose is to raise your awareness of defences. The *speaker* chooses to explore a workplace issue for up to three minutes. At each intervention by the *listener*, the *speaker* attempts to respond *tangentially* (for inspiration, think of the character Vicky Pollard in TV's *Little Britain*). The purpose of the exercise is to develop a chain of *tangents*. At the conclusion of the exercise the *listener*, *speaker*, and *observer* report what they saw, heard, and experienced.

Now, repeat the exercise, but this time the *listener* attempts to resist any temptation to engage in tangential transactions, focusing instead on drawing the *speaker* back to the present issue from the perspective of Adult awareness. The exercise can be repeated using blocking strategies for the *speaker* (*prevaricating*, *intellectualising*, or *blathering*) where the *listener* can begin to experiment with using their capacity to simply *notice* these behaviours and gently inquire about their use. Finally, discuss your experiences of working with the two types of defensive transactions.

Rewriting our scripts: It's never too late to have a happy childhood

Past, present and future are linked. The smell of freshly cut grass has always had a powerful effect on me. Possibly on you, too? It reminds me of long, hot summer days as a child, either making hay with family on our farm in the West of Ireland, or playing football in the local park with brothers and friends. You can understand, then, just how the *smell* of freshly cut grass can transport me, not necessarily to a specific place or time, but to a set of emotions that I now recognise to be associated with play, freedom, and, well, flourishing. I wasn't terribly aware of what a whiff could conjure up when, as an indifferent teenager, I visited a research laboratory for the first time on a school trip. On that particular day someone must have been working with benzaldehyde (it smells like freshly cut grass!) just before we arrived. On entering the laboratory I had the "freshly brewed coffee" experience so beloved by estate agents, and I was sold on organic chemistry from that moment on.

Now, the point of the story is not to suggest that I went into science just for the smells, but a smell alone was sufficient to trigger a powerful and, importantly, *positive* sensation from my past. What I am describing here is related to the idea of *transference*, which is understood as the re-experiencing of feelings, attitudes, fantasies, or defences in the here and now which may not fit the context because they originate from the past. In my example, a smell in the *present* led to the re-experiencing of an out-of-context sensation from my past. Similarly, a person in the present can trigger a memory of a significant other (i.e. a frightening or inconsistent carer) from our past. Transference is powerfully activated when we are in the presence of someone who feels significant to us in the here and now. For example, in the workplace this might include those who hold power over us, or control resources. TA is a useful framework for recognising emotional triggers in the here and now that can take us back to ways of thinking and feeling that may not always be positive, appropriate, or pleasant. The advantage of spotting hooks, or invitations to zoom back into our past and to think and feel as we once did, is that we can interrupt their unwelcome intrusion on the present.

Working with feelings and attitudes which do not belong to the present forms the core of our work as psychotherapists. Many, like myself, believe that our unhelpful past experiences, as understood through Berne's metaphorical ego states, are scripts from the past amenable to rewriting, not necessarily through a set of techniques but via self-awareness (see earlier, Johari rooms). It really is never too late to have a happy childhood.

When I have been triggered, I ignore features of the here and now, and instead replay an outdated definition of myself and others. It is a bit like looking in the mirror and instead of seeing the Adult, the 13-year-old version of *me* looks back. So by incorporating aspects of TA into our thinking, we can begin to recognise the triggers that cue outdated perspectives from our past. A key place to start is to notice bodily *sensations* that don't seem to match the context. For example, does my heart beat faster, is there a churning in my stomach or chest, or do I feel a lump in my throat in particular situations? Do I feel disconnected from the context, perhaps even feeling like I am watching myself in some scene from a drama? Maybe I talk faster than usual, my mouth feels dry, or I want to run away and hide or escape? Or perhaps, more alarmingly, I feel an overwhelming upsurge of anger, rage, or panic and anxiety?

With these ideas in mind, take a look at columns 1 and 2 of my *Workplace Trigger Diary* (Table 4.2). Here, I have noted a situation in the workplace that triggered what I felt was unusual for the setting. On reflection, I was reminded of thoughts and feelings associated with my past (i.e. column 3). It is OK for these sensations to be a little jumbled, because I am interested in noticing without interpreting for the time being. The associated *Drivers* add energy which intrudes on my here and now experiences. After saying more about these Drivers, you may wish to collect data and complete your own Workplace Trigger Diary, filling in column 4 as I have done.

The five characteristic driver styles. Do careful people-watchers become psychotherapists, or does the training hone our people-watching skills? What we can be sure of is that all theories of relationships have at their root careful observation and reflection on practice. This was certainly true of Taibi Kahler, who concluded that we possess a range of driver styles that help us get what we need from others (Stewart & Joines, 2012). In keeping with attachment theory, Kahler proposed that these *drivers* are deeply rooted in our emotional histories. Models that attempt to be neat and tidy rarely reflect the complexity of what it is to be human. Yet, you might recognise these *drivers* in yourself or others? I have added the corresponding *antidote* for each driver, which will hopefully diffuse its power over you (Hay, 2009):

- *Being perfect.* In our quest for perfection we have a reputation for producing accurate work. We are well organised because we look ahead and plan for problems. We are not taken by surprise because we have contingency plans ready. We are tempted to do everything ourselves because we do not trust others to do it right. In applying our high expectations we fail to recognise when "good enough" is OK, which makes us poor delegators. We like to follow what we say by counting off points on our fingers. We often speak parenthetically: "I would like to speak to you today, as I explained in my email, about possible restructuring of the team". *Antidote = I am already good enough.*
- *Pleasing others.* We find satisfaction in being appreciated for what we do for others. We are sympathetic, empathic, tolerant, and flexible. We seek to agree with others, avoiding conflicts at all costs because we are concerned about rocking the boat. We speak with a rising inflection at the end of our sentences (high rising terminal), and may wrinkle an eyebrow as we do so. Although we are good team members and nice to have around, we avoid conflict and worry about gaining approval to the extent that our own opinions and suggestions are so qualified that we seem to lack conviction. As we are reluctant to say NO, we allow others to interrupt us. We are likely to accept tasks from others instead of concentrating on our own priorities. *Antidote = It is OK to get my needs met.*
- *Being strong.* We feel energised by a crisis. It is when we get to feel useful. We actually enjoy being seen to do well under pressure. We are the ones who are able to stay logical when others are panicking, and remain emotionally detached from a situation, enabling us to problem-solve and deal efficiently with people who are angry or distressed. We can remain even-tempered and are consistent, which ensures others know what to expect from us. The problem is we hate admitting our weaknesses and can burn out before we ask for help. Deep down, we fear that we are unlovable, so we avoid asking for help for fear of being rejected. *Antidote = I am lovable even when I am vulnerable.*
- *Try harder.* The energy of people with this driver is at its highest when we have a new task to tackle, which is why managers love us – at first. Given a new project, we identify all the implications, including some that others

Table 4.2 Example of a workplace trigger diary

1 Situation and context	2 Corresponding sensations evoked	3 Childhood situations which come to mind Thoughts & Feelings	4 Unhelpful Drivers adding energy to the present
Preparing a presentation to give to my boss	Heart races and I can feel dread in my stomach	Memories of reciting my multiplication tables in front of the whole class – and I got it wrong! Will I be taken seriously? Fear of being shamed again	Being Perfect
A colleague doesn't finish a delegated task as quickly as I could – or at least that's what I think	Fizzing in my chest, irritation and tapping fingers	As the eldest child I was simply used to being a little faster and stronger when playing with my siblings. "I want to take over"	Hurry Up

may have overlooked. However, you can tell our initial interest wanes when we volunteer for new projects before we have finished the last. We spread our interests broadly, secretly making sure we do not succeed because our underlying motivation is to keep *trying. Antidote = I am already good enough.*

- *Hurry up.* People with this driver are motivated to work quickly and get a lot done in a short time. In fact we seem to enjoy having too much to do. But give us time to spare and we procrastinate until we find ourselves on the verge of a crisis. Whilst the ability to think quickly conveys the idea that we are impatient (finger tapping, darting eyes, watch checking, rushing words so that sometimes they tumble into each other) we actually don't take the time to plan. *Antidote = I will take my time because I am worth it.*

Returning to my workplace diary (Table 4.2), preparing a presentation for my boss perhaps triggers my *"Being perfect"* driver. I hear the voice of the *Critical Parent* (in fact, a mean teacher) who believed it was a good idea to use shame to motivate young people. In moments when my *Adapted Child* remembers this voice, my anxiety increases in a way that does not fit the context. An emotion from the past spills into the *present.* A pause to reflect allows me to operate from my Adult ego state. I recognise that my skills and abilities are already more than good enough to sail through the presentation. My Adult ego state has in effect reassured my Adapted Child. There is more than one way to tackle the second situation. The *"Hurry up"* driver is in fact an "I'm OK, you are *not*

OK" scenario. This might have been appropriate in my childhood when a little brother could not play with the older children, but a pause to listen to my Adult invites the question: "Do you provide colleagues with sufficient time to complete the task"?

The Drama Triangle

One of the most powerful ideas to emerge from TA is the *Drama Triangle*, which is particularly useful for understanding and then countering the disorientating and painful experience of emotional manipulation (Chapter 7). We instinctively understand that the two faces of drama, namely tears and laughter, are deeply compelling. Our addiction to reality television, soaps, and the banal intrigues of celebrity culture indicate to me that we all enjoy a little titillation. Yet when vicarious drama is not enough, some of us create and then become the stars of our own psycho-drama. Perhaps you know somebody at work, or in your friendship or family group, who seems to conduct their lives as if they were in their own personal "soap opera"? The dramatic arc tends to follow the familiar routine of: "So *I* said this, and *he* said that, so *I* did this (the tit-for-tat can go on for a while as we build dramatic tension), then *he* … (important pause for dramatic effect) *did something surprising!*" The drama comes about through a switch in the expected behaviour of one or other of the actors. However, the Drama Triangle is not about entertainment. Developmentally, seeking and then successfully maintaining the undivided attention of a carer can be a matter of life or death (Chapter 3). After all, the noisiest chick in the nest gets the juiciest grub. If our earliest developmental needs were not met in a consistent and attuned manner, then as adults we may become seduced into dramas or rapid emotional switching to get the attention we crave. Stephen Karpman was perhaps the first to understand that we draw attention to ourselves and create dramas in our relationships through the use of cyclical, emotional role reversals (1968). We play out a limited number of characters drawn from an over-simplified, *fairy-tale* version of the world as we see it. In the context of TA, these roles are termed *Rescuer*, *Persecutor*, and *Victim*, which again we capitalise to distinguish inauthentic behaviours in the Drama Triangle from any wider meaning (Figure 4.4)

Rescuers generally mean well and operate from a position of genuine concern for others, but as the saying goes: "the road to hell is paved with good intentions". The attitude of the *Rescuer* is to view others negatively because they cannot be trusted to solve their own problems. As *Rescuing* means having to either *do* or *think* more than their fair share, it is not long before they feel resentful about having to keep saving you, the *Victim*, from calamities of your own making. Micromanagers are an archetypal example of the *Rescuer*, and when they are challenged about what they are up to, it often backfires because

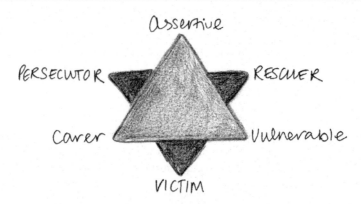

Figure 4.4 The Drama (Persecutor, Rescuer, & Victim) and the alternative Winners (Assertive, Carer, & Vulnerable) Triangle.

when *Rescuers* are not appreciated, they switch to feeling like an exploited *Victim*. This is a frustratingly powerless position to adopt because to feel better, others need to change. What they can do, however, is act either punitively or passively to conserve their resources of time and energy in preparation for the *switch* to *Persecutor*. Here, feeling better comes at the expense of the other in the classic zero sum game. In taking back power and satisfying their own needs, others are either passively or actively punished: "your lack of planning isn't my emergency, so sort yourself out". Once we enter the drama triangle, nobody gets to feel good for very long (see Box 4.6). However, we do have the option of using our positive ego states to either avoid being drawn into the psycho-drama, to step out of it if we are already in, or invite others out, and engage instead in a more authentic *Relational Approach*.

Box 4.6 *The Drama Triangle*

Carl worked on a part-time basis for several years because of childcare commitments. As the company expanded, they asked him to lead an important project for them, and as his family were now grown up he agreed to go full-time. Although the hours were long, things went well initially as Carl built his team. His painstaking attention to detail meant that the hours for him and his team were long, and he soon developed a reputation for running a "tight ship". He noticed that certain colleagues were not working to his exacting standards, and to save time he would often step in and take over. Supportive monitoring soon developed into micromanagement of certain colleagues, who were all, troublingly, female. He would undermine team members publicly and reassign projects to favoured individuals. Because this required even more of Carl's valuable time, resentment built on his part. Rumours began to circulate that Carl would become angry and even hostile in one-to-one meetings with colleagues, but he could remain relatively composed and plausible when there were others around. Team morale suffered, however, and complaints were made to HR. Some key members of the team left the company. However, Carl's response to any management concerns was to redouble his commitment by working even harder. He developed a habit of sending (and expecting responses to) emails in the early hours. This drew the attention of his line manager, who acknowledged that although Carl was entitled to work flexibly, for the sake of his health he should send emails during normal working hours. Carl stuck to the guidelines for a while, but the impact of his nocturnal habits soon began to take its toll on his health. Carl eventually stepped back from his full-time role, then a year later left the company.

Can you identify Carl's potential drivers? Do you recognise any switches in Carl's dramatic roles?

The *Relational Approach* and the Winner's Triangle. The three positions of the Drama Triangle namely *Rescuer*, *Persecutor*, and *Victim*, have alternatives that correspond to the Winner's Triangle (Choy, 1990; Burgess, 2005; Figure 4.4). Together, they give us a dynamic, star-shaped framework for thinking about our relationships. The *Rescuer* can choose the alternative *Carer* position by acknowledging and prizing the autonomy of those they otherwise think of as *Victims*. The role of *Persecutor* can be seen instead as being *Assertive*, which means actioning the fact that we *do* matter. Being *Vulnerable* – like a *Victim* – is unfortunately associated with being seen as powerless and weak, qualities we would rather hide from others and deny in ourselves. Yet the capacity to engage in a rational audit of our emotional world requires self-awareness, congruence, and authenticity; characteristics I see as being far from shameful. Being open to self-questioning in a gentle, curious, non-critical way is the beginning of understanding that we are worthy of love and respect *because* of our imperfections.

Assertive, *Carer*, and *Vulnerable* roles define the alternative Winner's Triangle. They defy manipulation, and are about being attuned to what is right for us and responsible *to* and not *for* others. I want now to examine Carl's psychodrama in Box 4.6, and ask whether a *Relational Approach* could have given the actors involved opportunities to engage in the alternative Winner's Triangle.

Caring not Rescuing. Both these roles have in common a genuine concern for others, but they differ in that *Carers* really do believe that people can think and feel for themselves, and understand that if they want help, they will ask for it. They do not take over unless they are asked. *Carers* are also clear about their boundaries. They assertively decline to be available to others if they do not want to be, or if they do not have the resources to do so. They are also clear about who benefits from doing things like offering reassurance, because they are careful about managing the expectations of others. *Carers* are also good at monitoring the boundaries of their time, the extent and purpose of their personal disclosures, and the use of their resources in the service of others. Carl clearly experienced difficulty in delegating work to others, perhaps because of his "Be perfect" driver. Acknowledging his drivers and finding the time to listen to members of his team could have helped Carl adjust his expectations and learn to trust his colleagues.

Vulnerable not Victim. Both positions are associated with feeling distressed, yet the former accesses Adult thinking to recognise how drivers such as "Be strong" can sabotage help-seeking. For Carl, initiating a discussion with his line manager about his anxiety with transitioning from part- to full-time working could have helped him access the self-care or support he needed. *Carers* recognise that the *Vulnerable* role requires both thinking *and* feeling, which means giving others the space to solve their own problems. Rather than taking over, Carl could have supported his team by asking: "What have you tried? How did that work? What went right/wrong? What next? How will you look after yourself if things go wrong?" Perhaps when Carl felt "short-changed" by some of the team because he was doing too much for them, it triggered thoughts about whether *his* needs were being met. Questions about barriers to delegation may have helped. Having the self-awareness to be who we really are at a given moment in a way that does not disempower others is the surest way to escape the Drama Triangle.

Assertive not Persecuting. Both have at their heart a desire to use our energy to get our needs met and to defend our dignity. However, the difference is that the former does not need to be punitive in achieving this. Being *Assertive* means asking for what we want, saying *no* to what we do not want, providing feedback about behaviour that is causing us problems, and explaining *why* it is a problem. Being *Assertive* means we no longer blame the other because our needs are not being met. Both *Assertive* and *Persecutor* can upset people and cause distress, but the former does so to change the status quo and get their needs met. Perhaps an *Assertive* stance by Carl's team could have led to some authentic feedback about relational dynamics, and how they felt undermined in their work. Congruence invites more congruence, and this is the way to challenge positively the status quo.

Things to keep in mind

- Berne's notion of Adult, Child, and Parent ego states bring into awareness how the past affects the present, and proposes practical ways to widen our repertoire of relating styles.
- Thinking about encounters as Transactions gives us an alternative vantage point from which to examine how we *do* relationships.
- The triad method is a practical tool for discovering what others think of us, and what we think of ourselves. It broadens our emotional spotlight to reveal more of our blind spots so we can develop a more realistic picture of *how* we are understood by others.
- Hooks, triggers, and drivers need not draw us into compelling psychodramas. A *Relational Approach* offers us choices about other ways of relating: *Caring* not *Rescuing*, *Vulnerable* not *Victim*, and *Assertive* as opposed to *Persecuting*.

Suggested answers to Box 4.2: 1 [i, A; ii, C; iii, P]; 2 [i, P; ii, A; iii, C]; 3 [i, C; ii, A; iii, P]; 4 [i, P; ii, A; iii, C]; 5 [i, P; ii, P; iii, A].

References

Adams JR. (2009). Using Winnie the Pooh characters to illustrate the transactional analysis ego states. *Journal of Creativity in Mental Health*, 4, 237–248.

Burgess RC. (2005). A model for enhancing individual and organisational learning of "emotional intelligence": The drama and winners' triangles. *Social Work Education*, 24(1), 97–112.

Choy A. (1990). The Winner's Triangle. *Transactional Analysis Journal*, 20(1), 40–46.

Gallrein AMB, Carlson EN, Holstein M, & Leising D. (2013). You spy with your little eye: People are "blind" to some of the ways in which they are consensually seen by others. *Journal of Research in Personality*, 47, 464–471.

Hay J. (2009). *Transactional Analysis for Trainers*. Hertford: Sherwood Publishing.

Karpman S. (1968). Fairy tales and script drama analysis. *Transactional Analysis Bulletin*, 7(26), 39–43.

Kirschenbaum H. (2007). *The Life and Works of Carl Rogers*. Monmouth: PCCS Books.

Luft J & Ingham H. (1955). *The Johari Window, a graphic model for interpersonal relations*. Los Angeles: University of California, Los Angeles.

Spice CG & Spice WA. (1976). A triadic method of supervision in the training of counselors and counseling supervisors. *Counselor Education and Supervision*, 15(4), 251–258.

Stewart I & Joines V. (2012). *TA Today: A New Introduction to Transactional Analysis*. Nottingham: Russell Press Ltd.

Villeré MF. (1981). *Transactional Analysis at Work*. New York: Prentice Hall Inc.

Chapter 5

Democratic working relationships

The egalitarian workplace

Vertical *coercion*. An implicit assumption of hierarchies is that we *need* a strong leadership caste to guide us, to shape our collective meaning, provide direction, and instruct us in what to value and believe. Top-down decision-making excludes the majority of people in the workplace from having a say about changes that affect them, contrary to the values of respect and autonomy consistent with a *Relational Approach*. The majority of us are largely exempt from defining the problem, analysing the options, and proposing a solution. Instead of genuine consultation, workers are subjected to a reactive process *after* a decision has been made and compliance is sought. Hierarchies are also just not *cool* now, especially in the creative industries where it is recognised that the punitive *Parent* ego state subjugates the creative, innovative playful *Child*. Seeing leadership as an organisational process and not something residing in an individual requires a shift of power: *less managing down, more representing up*. An organisation truly interested in wellbeing understands how a *Relational Approach* respects the autonomy and agency of its workers, and is prepared to reflect non-defensively on how it goes about its business. Before examining approaches to a more egalitarian workplace based on horizontal or peer influencing, I want to untangle the overlapping yet separate roles of manager and leader, which usually exert their authority downwards.

Manager or administrator roles are about controlling not inspiring, and using positional power to allocate resources, identify tasks, come up with job descriptions, and realise objectives with deadlines and budgets. They seek to exert *control* over what we do, and how we behave. The work is not visible, and goes on in private spaces behind closed doors with other, similarly invisible, managers, which means that it is shady and potentially corrupt. They exercise their coercive power in two subtle and sometimes ethically questionable ways.

Rewards for the compliant worker can include preferential allocation of nice offices/gadgets, undemanding tasks, scarce resources, and of course success in the labyrinthine processes of career progression where promotion does not necessarily mean a worker is more talented, creative, organised, visionary, insightful, etc. than their peers. It usually signals compliance and does not augur well for their willingness to challenge the *Corruption Complex* that I introduce later in Chapter 7.

Punitive action (or indeed *inaction*) extends to the use of soft power and includes closer monitoring, assigning less desirable tasks, having resources subtly diverted away from the non-compliant worker, and it goes without saying, promotion and career progression become elusive.

Many could not imagine their organisations without a specialised, professional manager caste to focus and monitor resources. However, a much-needed function is imbued with corruptible privileges and equally corruptible individuals, rendering a revolving-role approach unappetising for those who already enjoy having their hands on the levers of power. Individuals striving for power, accumulating more and more responsibility and thus undermining democratic processes, are not only tolerated in hierarchical organisations, they are enabled and lauded through the concept of a *career* (Diefenbach, 2019). This persistent and mesmerizing construct legitimises the actions of those who imagine, as we all do occasionally, that we will feel better about ourselves if we get that promotion, earn a bit more cash, and impress the impressionable.

Leadership, on the other hand, is about influencing, both horizontally and vertically, what we *feel* and *think*; it can be summarised by that now-discredited phrase, *hearts and minds*. It is about providing inspiration, encouragement, support, coordination, and feedback. Very few managers come close to meeting the lofty ideals of *both* managerial competence and visionary, ethical, and relationally skilful leadership. The Holy Grail for most HR advisers is to appoint/recruit relationally skilful and ethical managers who are *also* compliant; like the mythical goblet itself, it is a futile quest for an illusory quarry. Those at ease with depersonalising strategic plans and spreadsheets freeze like rabbits in the headlights of an oncoming truck when encountering a challenge to their relational *soft skills*, squealing: "I didn't sign up for this". Equally, a leader who consistently offers a *Relational Approach* cannot sustain the incongruence of viewing workers with little inherent value beyond their contribution to organisational outcomes. So how about a pragmatic approach? *Why expect technical management skills* and *exemplary relational behaviours from mere mortals?* As a Danish psychotherapist explained to me: "The secret of happiness? Keep your expectations low". So let us ask *less* of our managers/leaders, and *more* of our peers.

Horizontal *influencing*. Leaders need followers. It is we, the followers, who make up the majority of people at work, and who contribute the most to an organisations success (Kelly, 1992). Not everybody in an organisation wants to be a vertically aligned manager, leader, or follower, for that matter. At best, many of us tolerate our leaders or at worst, do not take them as seriously as they would like. Bureaucracy is about *mistrust*, a relational dynamic that sucks the life-giving force of creativity bone dry. The polar opposite of a bureaucracy is the nimble, enriching, flat "boss-free" anarcho-syndicate exemplified by the successful *Valve Corporation*. Such arrangements rely on horizontal peer-to-peer working and spontaneous ordering to emerge in response to new internal/external challenges or opportunities (Lee & Edmondson, 2017). Even in the most rigid and *uncool* organisations, effective mechanisms for horizontal working already exist. Management theorist Mats Alvesson reminds us that we already get our inspiration and support from alternatives to the vertical manager/leader arrangement (Alvesson & Blom, 2018). Peer influencing, uniquely characterised by the absence of vertical or hierarchical relationships, must become recognised, and even privileged as part of our work experience.

Are you a hierarchy junky? You may be surprised to learn of your already high levels of autonomy and independence from formal leadership networks at work. Take a moment to consider the networks you currently use for professional or personal development, advice, feedback and encouragement. Your involvement with the local branch of your trade union, the regular contact you have with former colleagues, leaders or managers, formal and informal mentors across the organisation, a supervisor, or peers within the same area of work but in a separate organisation. Let us not forget the wise counsel of our family and friends also. Professional bodies such as my own [i.e. the British Association for Counselling and Psychotherapy (BACP)] offer strong extended networks, a co-created ethical framework and code of practice, regular networking conferences, and continuing professional development. Conversely, with fewer lateral relationships in your working life you may already feel somewhat dependent on the politically savvy leader of your cabal (Chapter 7) or line manager. Developing alternative support networks separate from the formal structures in your organisation could mean that an inexperienced manager or leader feels that their authority and knowledge will be undermined, devalued, or challenged. The confident, trusting manager or leader will understand that peer influencing is flexible, knowledge-laden, free, and overall balanced and impartial.

In this chapter, I want to explore egalitarian working relationships characterised by an absence of vertical power. *Goal-oriented* relationships are important to us because they focus on *change*. They are interesting because although they incorporate key aspects of a *Relational Approach*, the person using such skills always has an agenda and that risks exploitation. I discuss safeguards against exploitation in our relationships towards the end of the chapter. *Mentoring* is a form of relationship often deployed in organisations to support people in adjusting to new roles. They are horizontal in terms of power, and I discuss how these partnerships sometimes mirror the difficulties we experience in our romantic relationships. Finally, I address *supervision*, or less formally the provision of a facilitated reflective space, which I believe to be necessary for all of us working in relationally challenging activities.

The goal-oriented relationship

Making up your mind to change. Goal-oriented relationships can help resolve inner struggles and mobilise resources to help us make staggeringly complex changes to our lives. In the workplace, we often seek to do something similar, which is to either change our own behaviours, or influence others to make a change that is important to the organisation or us. I want to introduce *Motivational Interviewing* (MI) here because of its growing popularity outside healthcare, where it is routinely used to stop behaviours that cost the taxpayer money, e.g. smoking, over-eating, and non-adherence to drug regimens. Employers are seeing the potential of MI to support people back to work after long-term sick leave, for example, because it is more cost-effective than replacing them (Ståhl & Gustavsson, 2018). The moral ambiguity of the goal-oriented relationship lies in its potential to pathologise the individual who needs to change, so distracting us from a system that is potentially doing harm (Chapter 8). You may also be interested in how MI could be used to help resolve the ambiguities of whether we leave our jobs or organisations. The so-called *fur-lined rut* is cosy, but a rut nevertheless.

Box 5.1 Change as a process

1. *Pre-contemplation*: This is when I start to experience the sensation of stuckness, even when others around me have known for some time that I need to change.
2. *Contemplation*: When I begin to acknowledge that my behaviour or attitudes are unhelpful – I recognise I need to change.
3. *Preparation*: I decide to change, and I make a plan.
4. *Action*: The action plan is in place, and change begins to happen.
5. *Maintenance*: Although change has happened, maintenance is required to avoid relapse.

As most psychotherapists would attest, the process leading up to and including the moment when change actually begins to happen is notoriously fragile and often sabotaged by our own resistance, fear, and anxiety. The MI approach stems from Bill Miller and Steve Rollnick's work with problem drinkers (2013), and James Prochaska and Carlo DiClemente's complementary ideas (1982) of change as a *process* (Box 5.1).

The MI approach focuses on the precarious pre-contemplation *and* contemplation phases where we ask, "Why should I change now?" Here, we are interested in mobilising our innate and underlying capacity for change, which shares key aspects of a *Relational Approach* in that it acknowledges our own expertise and wisdom. Stage models assume that by stepping on one rung of the ladder we develop the coping skills to move up to the next rung, but as any ex-smoker will tell you, we rarely go *cold turkey*. Relapse is part of the process, baby! We slip back to earlier stages, several times perhaps, skipping stages before finally achieving our goal and even then, vigilance is required; but importantly we never relapse as the same person.

At the heart of the MI approach is the resolution of our ambivalence between the perceived costs and benefits of changing complex and intractable behaviours. The experience of being stuck can be summarised by a statement like, "a part of me wants to change, but something holds me back". It would be nice to believe that the gap between our values and how we act produces a tension (incongruence, or surface acting) whose resolution leads to change. Yet, smokers who understand the health statistics and can calculate (and then ignore) the financial costs of their habit continue to huddle together outside our public buildings even in the most horrible weather. It is never about the statistics, because we only quit habitual behaviours when we understand we can manage our emotions without them. Although MI is often promoted as a manualised technique involving listening skills (see OARS in Box 5.2), the emotional aspect of the change process demands an authentic *Relational Approach*.

Box 5.2 OARS

- *Open questions* are a good way to start a discussion about why change is useful. They are easy to recognise because it is difficult to answer one with a straight yes or no! For example, "what are the good things that might happen if you could work with Tina?"
- *Affirming* is about communicating positive regard for the speaker. In a clinical setting, for example, a counsellor is especially committed to recognising and acknowledging the courage it takes to seek help. Seemingly small successes must be noticed and celebrated.
- *Reflection* is a powerful skill that communicates that you have an accurate understanding of what is *meant*. Externalising thoughts and feelings without having our world view (as it stands) challenged or judged is something we rarely experience. It is frustrating to externalise my inner world only for a well-meaning listener to play devil's advocate. This is *zero-sum* relating, which blocks and undermines communication, and says *you must be wrong so I can get to be right*.
- *Summary* statements gather key ideas that have emerged during the discussion. For example, they could say something about a person's desire ("Part of me knows I can't go on like this ...") or ability ("I guess I could meet with her and see how it goes ...") to change.

The transformational power of a *Relational Approach*. A core assumption of MI shared with a *Relational Approach* is *I trust you to know what is right for you*. A powerful predictor of success for MI is the capacity to convey both our suspension of disbelief and our active curiosity about the speaker's perspectives and resistance to change. A *Relational Approach* is incompatible with the idea that we see ourselves as the expert, viewing the speaker from a deficit perspective, which is to say: *you lack the insight, knowledge or skill to know what is best for you* (e.g. *The Rescuer* – Chapter 4). It makes little sense offering a relationship that honours the wisdom of the speaker if you believe that your version of wisdom must be installed first. Offering advice, insight, psycho-education, or coaching when ambivalence remains only triggers resistance. This is not to say that signposting is not useful or indeed essential when someone has already made the decision to change, but offering tools for change too early in the process can backfire.

The reduction of MI to a set of manualised methods to be repeated parrot fashion has led to problems establishing the evidence base for its effectiveness. Yet astonishingly, researchers continue to overlook the transformative power of a *Relational Approach* when applied to MI (Moyers, 2014). It requires patience and practice, and because of our default attachment strategies the *Relational Approach* is more easily acquired by some than others. Yet it is required when working with *change talk*, and *resistance*, which I describe next (Box 5.3).

Box 5.3 The goal-oriented relationship

Six months after joining the company, Andy was signed off work with stress. Tina, his line manager, extended his probation to accommodate his recovery. However, eight months later, Andy is refusing to talk with Tina. He recently joined the union, and in his first meeting with Harriet, his representative, he begins exploring the impact of his stress. The goal for Harriet in this complex situation is to support Andy to re-engage with Tina so they can resolve their impasse.

Amplifying change talk

C(1): *I don't want to talk to Tina ... she hates me ... is it any wonder I'm so stressed? My son has to see me like this ... it's wrong.*

H(1): *How your son sees you is important too ... I hear that ... and you don't want him to be affected by what you are experiencing.*

C(2): *I must get over this for his sake really ... I have to face up to what it is about Tina that bothers me.*

H(2): *So … if you can talk to Tina it just might make things easier at home?*

C(3): *Yeah … maybe I could meet her and see how it goes … as long as you are in the room she's unlikely to be horrible to me … that might work.*

H(3): *Don't worry … I'll be there to look after you.*

Rolling with resistance

C(4): *You see, I don't think Tina wants me back. She picked on me from the start.*

H(4): *That is a horrible situation to be in … feeling pushed out when you just want to belong … and it's interesting how you reacted by withdrawing further.*

C(5): *Hmmm (less angrily now, and more thoughtful) … can you blame me?*

H(5): *It certainly sounds like you find it difficult to work with her … ideally though … you would keep your job but leave your boss … have I got that right?*

C(6): *I love the work … I need to find a way of getting along with Tina … I guess?*

Amplifying change talk. The MI relationship is strategically focused on speech that reflects the desire, ability, or commitment to change. The interviewer is vigilant for opportunities to reinforce the speaker's fragile process by nurturing the green shoots that suggest a readiness to change. I am not so naïve to believe that speech alone triggers change. However, in the same way that a tree in a parched landscape is a sign of water, so change talk is a signal of growing self-efficacy.

Our union caseworker Harriet is using the MI approach in her work with Andy (Box 5.3). She invites exploration by Andy through a simple reflection [H(1)] that spontaneously leads to commitment talk (I must …) about his son and how this could motivate engagement with line manager Tina. Harriet extends Andy's thinking with an open question [H(2)] inviting further exploration of the argument for change. Once Andy is ready to discuss change, it would be counter-productive to return to exploring his motivation. Now is the time to be curious about how Andy sees change happening, and what unique contributions he can make to that change. We all need time to get used to the idea of change before we can commit to it. It is tempting here for Harriet to take over and *Rescue* Andy with [H(3)] (i.e. *Drama Triangle*, Chapter 4) rather than adopt a healthier *Carer* role that respects Andy' autonomy and self-efficacy.

Rolling with resistance. It can be useful to amplify change talk, but it is far more powerful to understand how we work effectively with resistance. When we experience challenges to our argument *against* changing something it only reinforces our sense of conflict and ambivalence. This is an example of *zero-sum* relating that wastes energy and time because for me to win then you, the speaker, must lose. Here, the *interviewer* must resist any need to be "right", trusting the speaker to work through the process under his or her own steam. For example, when Andy talks about Tina being a "nightmare", Harriet must park her own experience of having worked with the adorable Tina for several years.

The strategies for *Rolling with Resistance* are mostly variations on the skill of reflection. Amplification, for example, is when we overstate the speaker's resistance, and Harriet combines this with noticing a contradiction in how Andy sees things [H(4)]. Andy does not need to waste time and energy getting Harriet to understand his perspective. Instead, he begins to reflect on the ambiguity at the heart of his attachment; he wants to belong, yet feels compelled to withdraw (Chapter 3).

Another approach sees Harriet use a reflection that focuses on Andy's ambivalence. By making choices more concrete we emphasise Andy's sense of autonomy [i.e. H(5) − C(6)]. By avoiding *zero-sum* relating, Harriet joins with the resistance and comes alongside Andy rather than going head-on. Harriet's *Relational Approach* means she can put her pride to one side and resist the temptation to be right, or even worse, be righteous. Instead, she trusts Andy to voice his resistance and avoid the difficult and unnecessary work of diffusing this anger later.

The next section considers relationships that also have an outcome in mind, but when compared to a goal-orientated encounter, mentoring tends to be much more diffuse in its intended outcomes, and at its best is especially characterised by the co-created nature of the relationship.

Support through mentoring

The search for a secure base at work. You may have already benefitted from informal mentoring, perhaps remembered as the steady kindness of someone older, probably long gone, and not sufficiently thanked? You will already understand, then, the importance of seeking out someone to give you that sense of everyday belonging. Someone who, in times of stress, understands, reassures, and comforts. A generous or inspiring colleague whose door is always open. An experienced and admired peer, perhaps, willing to take the time to discuss frustrations or concerns over a coffee without needing first to tell you about their day? Someone who goes out of their way to tell you they have faith in your ability to meet a challenge. There are unintended learnings, too. An influential figure in my early days as a scientist told me with a twinkle in his bloodshot eyes: "weekdays are for keeping up, weekends are for getting ahead": I have remained clear-eyed about my own work–life balance ever since.

Formal mentoring is a developmentally focused relationship between two people in the same organisation. It often involves a senior or experienced *insider* (mentor) and a less experienced or junior mentee (protégé), usually outside the mentor's line of supervisory or management influence. The mentee develops both personally and professionally, and this differs from coaching which focuses only on skills specific to an aspect of performance in a job. The benefits of *formal* mentoring are largely a matter of faith, as there is only a weak link between being a mentee and positive outcomes such as job satisfaction, organisational commitment, a lower desire to leave, and higher rates of pay and promotion (Eby, 2012). The benefits for a mentor are thought to be generative and similar to those of becoming a parent, an experience that changes our relationship with a future that will not involve us. We return to generative tasks and the satisfaction we get from developing others such as legacy building later in Chapter 8. As formal mentoring involves settling someone in, or socialising them into a new role, it tends to be fixed-term, and evolves through the stages of *initiation, maturation,* and *decline*. Just as with romantic relationships, there can be a shadow side to the arranged mentoring dyad. Negative experiences and disappointments arise from a mismatch in attitudes and values, leading to deception, jealousy, and even betrayal. *Initiation* is like any arranged coupling where some third party decides how the needs of the organisation are best met. Little attention is given to the couple's compatibility, even though such considerations predict a successful and nurturing relationship (Hu *et al.*, 2016).

Informal mentoring, on the other hand, is initiated by either mentor or mentee, and is usually driven by their respective needs and wants (Janssen *et al.*, 2016). Informal arrangements often go unrecognised or are not articulated so are less visible to the gaze of the organisation, or researchers for that matter. These informal relationships *mature* easily, and are experienced as more intense than formal arrangements because its scope is unbounded, with the focus extending beyond professional to personal development.

It is true of both formal and informal relationships that the mentee ultimately outgrows aspects of their mentor's guidance, and the relationship enters the stage of *decline*. The mentor in their turn may also conclude they have done all they can to develop the mentee. Here, the mentor–mentee coupling mirrors how dependence cools in the parent–adolescent relationship. Like a teenager, the attachment needs of a mentee do not stop, but simply shift to groovier peers. Unfortunately, researchers in the field of mentoring continue to see the dyad as little more than an instrumental social exchange. This reductionist approach allows little room to acknowledge our human needs and the transformational power of a *Relational Approach*.

Mentoring, attachment, and a *Relational Approach*. Mentoring relationships are a powerful opportunity for personal development because they are where our unhelpful ways of working with fear, anger, and shame can become apparent. Secure and low levels of anxious/avoidant attachment are compatible with developmentally effective mentoring relationships because participants seek intimacy and enjoy exploring the balance between closeness and autonomy. Here, feedback becomes an exciting opportunity to integrate new learning about others and ourselves. We capitalise on *good-enough* mentoring, learning to handle setbacks without catastrophising, or ruminating negatively about missed appointments, or clumsy/careless feedback, etc. (Gormley, 2008; Wang *et al.*, 2009).

Anxious attachment strategies become problematic for a *mentee* who is hypervigilant about rejection by their mentor, responding strongly to perceived slights. The cycle of testing the security of the relationship begins through clingy help-seeking, such as expecting support when autonomy would be more appropriate. Resentment and anger can trigger a self-defeating withdrawal from the relationship because we sense it cannot safely contain our strong feelings without irreconcilable consequences.

A *mentor's* awareness of default attachment strategies provides them with a richer menu of options at critical moments when the downwards spiral of withdrawal beckons. For the mentor, an apparent lack of commitment by a mentee might ordinarily deter them from investing further in the relationship. Fewer or lower-quality encounters become a self-fulfilling prophecy for both, as mutual withdrawal takes hold. The mentor who notices the withdrawal dynamic can instead offer consistency, patience, and through a *Relational Approach*, invite the mentee back from the brink of their grumpy self-imposed isolation. An anxious *mentor* finds it difficult to handle the growing autonomy of their mentee, preferring instead to engage in *Rescuing* behaviours such as intrusive micromanagement, unwanted contact, or risky boundary transgression (i.e. *The Drama Triangle* – Chapter 4). A significant majority of those reporting sexual or emotional violations in mentoring relationships arise from anxious dynamics where partners become seduced into believing that the relationship can meet *all* their needs.

Avoidant strategies are all about keeping the peace, so unsurprisingly we deflect situations that could lead to conflict or even intimacy. Because we do not draw attention to our needs, problems for a mentee become the ball kicked into the long grass: "well, I didn't want to make a fuss". Avoidant strategies deter us from engaging in developmentally useful help-seeking behaviour, seeing the risks of dropping our defences as outweighing the benefits of inviting a *Relational Approach*.

Mentees unaware of their default avoidant strategy will see their mentors as cool, aloof, and unavailable, even when objective outsiders see them as being supportive. We become mistrustful of our mentor's good intentions, seeing caregiving as creepy rather than the benign benevolence intended.

A *mentor* who defaults to avoidant strategies may be more interested in meeting the practical or strategic career functions of the role rather than any psychosocial or relational skills development. They may come across as aloof, remote, or even defensive, preferring instead to project a "professional" or enigmatic persona to their mentees. When both parties engage in avoidant strategies, the relationship falls fallow. In professions where technical skills are prized above social, a match of avoidant partners may be tolerable. A technically brilliant manager in a scientific setting responsible for mentoring "apprentices" (PhD and postdoctoral workers) sought to project an aloof Professorial persona to "keep things simple". Distracted by publications and self-aggrandisement, he was unable to see just how low morale was, and how it was leading to high turnover in his team. In a helping profession, such a match would be dysfunctional and perhaps perilous to those in the care of the team.

We have few opportunities to develop competency in mentoring before we actually do it – we learn on the job. Entering a relationship where we are trusted with the development of a person brings with it the potential for abuse and exploitation: it requires supervision and ethically informed behaviour, which we discuss next.

The container of supervision

Who is it for and what does it do? Supervision is for you if you are involved in challenging communications with people, or relationally complex and emotionally difficult work (BACP, 2018). This includes people such as managers, leaders, mentors, or anyone involved in goal-oriented relationships where the potential for the abuse or misuse of power and trust exists. This guiding principle encompasses those of us who spend our days with anxious or demanding people; for instance, in healthcare and educational settings. It also applies to those of us who offer compassion to the emotionally distressed, despairing, or psychologically troubled. We often overlook the emotional impact of working with angry and traumatised people in our correctional institutions, on the front line of maintaining order with unreasonable or abusive members of the public, and helping the homeless or the destitute. All this emotional labour requires the support of supervision, or a less-formal facilitated reflective space that can be offered either one-to-one or in a group.

We also need support beyond the initial training we get when we start out. Supervision as a process fosters learning, development, and wellbeing as we try to do our best work. Burnout is the depletion we experience through excessive emotional labour and is signalled by a lack of concern about what we do and cynicism about those who we are there to work with. The dead-eyed indifference of the colleague who has given too much is perhaps familiar to many. Repeated and constant exposure to emotional pressure over a prolonged period ultimately leads to the painful realisation that we have nothing left to give.

Counsellors and psychotherapists rely on formal and informal support to stay alert to the ethical and emotional demands of complex and occasionally competing roles. My own supervision is independent of line management.

I require confidentiality, safety, and containment around what I do to remain psychologically healthy in my various roles as counsellor, supervisor, trainer, trade union caseworker, colleague, husband, father, son, brother, and friend. My supervisory relationships keep me vigilant about the illusions, delusions, and possible collusions in my work, so I can keep my feet on the ground. *It ensures my conscience remains my guide, and not my accomplice.* Supervision offers me the opportunity to stand back and reflect so I avoid the easy option of blaming colleagues, the organisation, or even myself, and recognise how important learning emerges from even the most difficult situations.

Being *good enough* at work. The psychoanalyst Donald Winnicott brought to our attention the importance of the mother–infant relationship through his concept of the *good enough* mother. A baby's emotional needs, like those of an organisation, can never be fully met. Containing my feelings of guilt or inadequacy whilst allowing my baby to rage and scream, my toddler to completely lose it, or an organisation to ask for more than I have to give, is hard to do unless I am supported by others. The primary triad formed between two parental figures and those who they care for has at its core a partnership that is solid enough to hold and contain even the wildest rages of one, or more, hungry infants. Similarly, supervision offers a container to hold the strong and complex emotions that others project onto me in the world of work (Merenda & Miano, 2015).

Supervision as a *container* for workplace distress. Organisations – especially those that help people in distress – become a receptacle for the displacement of other people's anger, fear, envy, narcissism, pride, uncertainty, and more. Those of us who work empathically will experience these emotions, often amplified, through emergent processes at work (see Chapter 6). That is to say, we can adopt similar emotions, thinking patterns, and behaviours to those who seek our help. Organisational representatives (i.e. managers or leaders) who are unaware of these projections amplify the impact of chronic stress in their organisations and the dysfunctional ways we adapt to them. We cope by defending ourselves through *rituals* that unfortunately solve nothing and only prevent us from thinking, feeling, and learning. This is not only to the detriment of our colleagues, but to the people who are the mission of our organisations (Bloom, 2011). The capacity of workers to healthily contain the emotions of these projected, parallel processes will depend on the self-awareness, emotional maturity, and level of supervision they receive.

Supervision, then, is not just an event, but an attitude that must permeate the culture of every helping organisation committed to its wellbeing, through the mediation and integration of stressful processes.

A Relational Approach to supervision. There is no fixed model to understand and negotiate the process of supervision involving an individual or even a group, although Chapter 6 explores some of the complexity of what emerges when we come together as a collective. However, the approach of Hawkins and Shohet (2012) stands the test of time because it is holistic and relational. It presumes that supervision is less about stages of development, intervention styles, key tasks or even monitoring, but more about layers of simultaneous processes. It is an approach committed to viewing the worker, the supervisor, and those they help (clients) in their widest possible context. Therefore, effective supervision is our opportunity to engage in seeing ourselves, our relationships, and their context through a range of superimposed and overlapping lenses that I describe next (Figure 5.1).

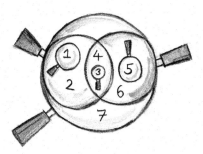

Figure 5.1 The lenses of supervision.

1. *Thinking about others.* The focus here is to enable me, the supervisee, to see what takes place when I am working with others. For example, how do others present themselves to me, what areas of their lives do they choose to explore, and what might they hide or defend against? The challenge here is to stick with what is said or seen, and not to speculate or be drawn into interpretation.

2. *My strategies and interventions in relation to others.* Interest here is not only in the choices I make in my work, but also why I make them and what influenced their timing. For example, if I choose to delay a meeting with someone I find difficult, what lay behind that decision?

3. *My own process.* The supervisor explores not only the conscious impact of my work, but edge-of-awareness dynamics that might influence my relationships. I might be encouraged to share fantasies about a colleague; perhaps they remind me of someone, say a teacher that frightened me at school. Is this why I avoid them?

4. *The relationship we co-create.* This tries to see beyond the previous three lenses, and explores instead what emerges in the relationships we co-create

(Chapter 6). Stepping out of my own perspective and seeing things as if from a distance, I can reflect on my projections or fantasies I put onto other people. Do I avoid someone because they remind me of an intimidating show-off from the playground? Could that person feel the need to show off because they want my attention? Could a different perspective help us work better together?

5. *The supervisor's process.* Attention shifts to their own experiencing of the supervision process. Here-and-now sensations for them in response to what I present is another source of information about what might be happening with my colleagues. The self-awareness of the supervisor prepares the ground for seeing through the next lens.

6. *The supervisory relationship.* The supervisor considers the *"here-and-now"* relationship with their supervisee, and examines parallels with the *"there-and-then"* working relationships of the supervisee. For example, my supervisor may notice how resistant I am to accepting how the show-off may be just like the Adapted Child who wants to be loved. Perhaps I too fear being unlovable?

7. *The context.* The focus so far has been on the supervisor–supervisee–client *triad* which exists in a wider context that influences us all. Working holistically means it is unrealistic to draw lines around the humanity of the triad, so sex, family, gender, age, race, personal styles, theoretical orientation, and organisational history, etc. all need to be added to the mix.

Safeguards against exploitation

The higher up the tree a monkey climbs … Vertical hierarchies are notoriously prone to corruption and exploitation because workers are monitored much less the higher up they climb. This is in contrast to flatter arrangements where managers compete against and monitor each other much more closely (Rosenblatt, 2012). The sheer scale of some organisations also divorces us from individual accountability for our roles, and promotes the practice of *bystanding* or "turning a blind eye" to things we know to be wrong (Chapter 7). We are all vulnerable to taking the easy way out because of pressures specific to our context. The long job interview, or acting-up as it is commonly termed, brings with it pressures to comply, compromising the foundations of an effective mentoring relationship. When seeking or offering support to change our behaviour, or in the case of mentoring and supervision, we must trust that the relationship is not being used to serve some other purpose that is not in our interest. Further ethical obligations are created for the mentor, supervisor, etc. in the exercise of their influence and expertise because we often seek support or guidance in times of stress or vulnerability. A commitment to being ethical is the only way to protect the interests of all involved if we hope to engage in a *Relational Approach* (Box 5.4; Bond, 2015).

Box 5.4 Relating ethically

- Whose interests are served by this relationship?
- Am I comfortable telling others in the organisation about what I am doing?
- Who benefits from what I am doing, or what I am offering?
- When the encounter has come to an end, whose expectations were met?

We are often wary of taking a "leap of faith" when it comes to trusting others, and not just at work. It perhaps explains why informal mentoring is more effective than formal arrangements, because we prefer to evaluate the integrity and trustworthiness of a potential supporter by checking out their relational track record by word of mouth. When matters of scale mean we cannot rely on word of mouth, what is it that guides the way we evaluate others? A published statement about an organisation's ethical commitment to its members helps. Because there are so many contexts in which our relationships take place, can we expect a single set of well-defined ethical rules to apply to all settings? When examining the ethical guidelines used by English-speaking bodies for counselling and psychotherapy, for example, it seems there are two broad approaches (Bond, 2015). *Rule-based* codes of practice are often specific and lengthy as they work on the assumption that what is not forbidden is allowed. This is why they resemble legal documents; they spell out the letter of the law. Such rule-based codes of practice require compliance and speak well to those fearful of taking responsibility for their roles. A more flexible *principle-based* approach focuses on action and values, offering more opportunities to think about what we do and why we do it. The principle-based approach is about asking: "can I justify and explain what I do?" In the absence of guidelines relevant to your specific context, you might consider adopting principles based on those used by the British Association for Counselling and Psychotherapy (Box 5.5).

Box 5.5 Ethical values

- Being trustworthy means honouring the promises we make.
- Acknowledging a colleague's right to know what is right for them.
- Avoiding doing harm to a colleague.
- Doing good means a commitment to promoting the wellbeing of others.
- Justice is about the fair and impartial treatment of others.
- Self-respect is all about the *Golden Rule* of reciprocity – you are entitled to all of the above.

The practice of working ethically. An ethical dilemma is by definition difficult to resolve perfectly; when you encounter such a challenge in a working relationship it is useful to approach its resolution in a systematic way, especially if it is in a stressful or time-limited situation (Bond, 2015). A step-wise process for optimising the likelihood of arriving at a solution you can be confident of is illustrated using the example of Sophie's dilemma when working with Boris and his various laptops (Box 5.6).

Box 5.6 Sophie's dilemma

Sophie is a union caseworker who stepped in at short notice to support Boris in a meeting with his manager. Although Sophie and Boris have never met, she is briefed beforehand and expects the meeting to be routine. However, it soon becomes obvious that the manager has something more serious to discuss. During an update of corporate IT, inappropriate materials were discovered on a laptop Boris had used on a business trip. The manager explained that whilst the materials were not illegal, they were in breach of company policy about acceptable use. As part of an internal investigation, Boris is asked to surrender a laptop currently on loan to him. He denies any impropriety, and explains that the laptop in his possession was stolen from his car. Confused and concerned, Sophie asks for a brief adjournment to consult with the member. During this private discussion, a flustered Boris mutters to himself: "I must get rid of the damn laptop when I get home". Sophie must now quickly decide how this disclosure affects both her working relationship with the member and her organisation.

---

1. *Describe the dilemma.* Boris seems to have been caught red-handed breaking company policy, and furthermore it sounds like he is attempting to cover his tracks by disposing of its property. How does Sophie support Boris *and* work ethically? Which ethical principles in Box 5.5 do you feel are relevant to Sophie?
2. *Whose dilemma is it anyway?* Boris has made or is about to make his own choices and decisions about past and future conduct. The dilemma is *his*.
3. *Consider your ethical responsibilities, principles, or guidelines.* Here, Sophie considers what actions are prohibited by law, what actions are required to be performed by law, and what rights and responsibilities the law protects. There is no indication that a law has been broken yet, despite Boris' disclosure, and there are no specific ethical guidelines for Sophie as a trade union representative. However, Sophie should be mindful of treating Boris

fairly and *impartially*, respecting his autonomy, promoting his best interests whilst adhering to her own requirement to be *trustworthy*.

4. *Select the best course of action.* Sophie advises Boris to cooperate with the investigation. Given his disclosure, she explains that she can no longer represent him, and will refer him back to his usual caseworker. Sophie suggests the meeting reconvene when his usual representative is available.

5. *Evaluate.* On reflection, Sophie was happy that she stepped back from what would have been an ethically compromising case. Boris continued to deny misuse of company systems, but the assembled evidence was overwhelming. Although the caseworker did the best they could, company policy was clear about such matters and Boris was dismissed accordingly.

Things to keep in mind

- Peer-to-peer influencing is characterised by the *absence* of vertical or hierarchical structures and is a uniquely powerful way to receive direction, support, coordination, inspiration, and feedback. Worker autonomy is an uncomfortable reminder to believers in Michel's *Iron Law* that in vertical hierarchies, managers need followers more than employees need managers.

- Supervision is recommended to anyone who works in a role that regularly requires engagement in emotionally challenging activities. If an organisation is serious about wellbeing, then it will see supervision not as an expense, but as an investment in its people and those they serve.

- Goal-oriented support, mentoring, or supervision offered without ethical guidelines risks exploitation and emotional abuse.

References

Alvesson M & Blom M. (2018). Beyond leadership and followership: Working with a variety of modes of organizing. *Organisational Dynamics*, 48, 28–37.

BACP (British Association for Counselling and Psychotherapy) (2018). Ethical Framework for the Counselling Professions, Good Practice Point 73 (July 2018).

Bloom S. (2011). Trauma-organised systems and parallel process. In N. Tehrani (Ed.), *Managing trauma in the workplace: Supporting workers and organisations*. Abingdon: Routledge.

Bond T. (2015). *Standards and ethics for counselling in action* (4th ed.). London: Sage.

Diefenbach T. (2019). Why Michels' 'iron law of oligarchy' is not an iron law – and how democratic organisations can stay "oligarchy-free". *Organization Studies*, 40(4), 545–562.

Eby LT. (2012). Workplace mentoring: Past, present, and future perspectives. In SWZ Kozlowski (Ed.). *The Oxford handbook of organizational psychology.* New York: Oxford University Press.

Gormley B. (2008). An application of attachment theory: mentoring relationship dynamics and ethical concerns. *Mentoring & Tutoring: Partnership in Learning,* 16(1), 45–62.

Hawkins P & Shohet R. (2012). *Supervision in the helping professions* (4th ed.). London: Sage.

Hu C, Wang S, Wang Y-H, Chen C, & Jiang D-Y. (2016). Understanding attraction in formal mentoring relationships from an affective perspective. *Journal of Vocational Behavior,* 94, 104–113.

Janssen S, van Vuuren M, & de Jong MDT. (2016). Informal mentoring at work: A review and suggestions for future research. *International Journal of Management Reviews,* 18, 498–517.

Kelly R. (1992). *The power of followership.* New York: Doubleday.

Lee MY & Edmondson AC. (2017). Self-managing organisations: Exploring the limits of less-hierarchical organizing. *Research in Organizational Behaviour,* 37, 35–58

Merenda A & Miano P. (2015). Co-parental couples and new families: A study of the primary triad. *Procedia – Social and Behavioural Sciences,* 174, 1107–1110.

Miller WR & Rollnick S. (2013). *Motivational interviewing: Preparing people for change* (3rd ed.). New York: Guilford Press.

Moyers TB. (2014). The relationship in motivational interviewing. *Psychotherapy,* 51(3), 358–363.

Prochaska JO & DiClemente CC. (1982). Transtheoretical therapy: Towards a more integrative model of change. *Psychotherapy,* 19(3), 279–288.

Rosenblatt V. (2012). Hierarchies, power inequalities, and organizational corruption. *Journal of Business Ethics,* 111, 237–251.

Ståhl C & Gustavsson M. (2018). Introducing motivational interviewing in a sickness insurance context: Translation and implementation challenges. *Journal of Occupational Rehabilitation,* 28, 357–364.

Wang S, Noe R, Wang Z, & Greenberger D. (2009). What affects willingness to mentor in the future? An investigation of attachment styles and mentoring experiences. *Journal of Vocational Behavior,* 74, 245–256.

Chapter 6

Groups and teams

Group process – awareness versus seduction

Thinking about work as a social activity. None of us thrive in isolation. The process of individuals coming together for some common purpose has formed the centrepiece of human social organisation since our ancestors first gathered in collectives to hunt, raise families, and stay safe. As far as work is concerned, if it did not already exist, then somebody would surely have invented it as a way for us to engage in a social activity. A *Relational Approach* emphasises how our wellbeing as individuals is entwined with that of our community, group, or team. To many, belonging to a group and attending lots of meetings is what makes work interesting, fun, and perhaps even therapeutic. For others, the prospect of spending time with people we would not otherwise choose to be with whilst working inefficiently towards a goal that does not interest us is our idea of hell. I suspect that for the majority of us being in a team or group at work falls somewhere between these two extremes. A *group* is by definition an assembly of people with some unifying social activity, interest, or quality. *Teams*, on the other hand, have many overlapping qualities with a group, but they have some specific purpose, especially in the workplace. I do not want to confuse matters and be bogged down by definitions, so I will continue to use the terms team and group interchangeably because what matters is that we understand that work is a social activity.

The democratic work team. The growing emphasis of *leadership* in the workplace brings with it the unspoken assumption that we are at our happiest when conforming to being a follower, which by implication requires the subordination and marginalisation of our capacity for critical thinking and reflection. Our heavy reliance on leadership and followership roles at work alienates those of us who choose not to belong solely to one camp. Workers can take matters into their own hands and view leadership as a shared process and not something that resides in a person. We accept as if it were some natural law the fact that people competent in a specialist task in their industry must be elevated to leadership positions. When they do this badly, along come the legion of consultants and trainers to motivate us to work better in the dysfunctional environments they create. The main theme introduced in the last chapter was that there are other ways for us to work together that do not rely on power residing in an individual. A humanistic approach is interested in richer and more diverse ways for us to offer and receive direction, support, coordination, inspiration, and feedback. Self-managing and self-organising teams or clans are far more productive, satisfying, and motivating for their members (Chapter 2). Systems of worker co-determination were adopted by large organisations in Germany from the 1970s to give employees influence in the decisions affecting their wellbeing as well as business direction. No system of worker participation can exist without a civic culture consistent with a *Relational Approach*, i.e. one with the shared values of democracy, trust, responsibility, and respect (Lee & Edmondson, 2017). In addition to the peer-to-peer working approaches discussed in the last chapter, I want to examine how all of us can participate in the democratic life of a group or team, through understanding the different styles of relating which challenge traditional, disempowering practices of bureaucracies.

When groups work well, members share responsibility, support each other, and learn from one another without too much interference from an external manager. Although groups are seldom rudderless, no single member need stand out in terms of their influence over others; all play a part in influencing the direction and boundaries in the group. The functional team may, of course, involve formal managers from time to time when, for example, matters of resourcing arise, but they are not pivotal to providing inspiration and vision. We recognise we are in a healthy group when discussions are rational, creativity abounds and knowledge and ideas flow freely. When things go well we may even be reminded of shared sand-play as infants, a place where leadership is *liquid*. Groups also offer an intimate setting for sharing our knowledge and ideas. Our voice feels small in a vast hierarchy where managers and leaders become attached to the notion that they alone must have all the best ideas. I am not so naïve to suggest that groups operate in this utopian manner, even for some of the time. I am, however, interested in examining what deflects teams and groups from working this way for even some of the time.

What gets in the way of team democracy? Irrespective of your emotional response to being in a team at work, you should be curious about why you may be deflected from what you meet to do. The perfect group is not easy to establish. We all have different expectations of leadership, control, and boundaries, so it is useful to reflect on what works for you. We have different ideas, values or interests that can lead to conflict or time-consuming and distracting discussions. People arrive late, or as is increasingly commonplace, members become distracted by their devices. What does this communicate? "I've got better things to do" or "I don't value you"? Disruptive habits go unchallenged because something stops us from doing this. Why is this so? In teams, we can also find ourselves compromising what we really feel and think as individuals. We find ourselves going along with what we do not believe in, remaining silent in the face of decisions and behaviours we do not like. It seems that groups take on a life of their own, which deflects us from the task in hand.

What is key here is whether you are interested in changing the way you do things. If so, then it is important to recognise that, especially so in groups, fear, anger, and shame get in the way. But by focusing on our *in the moment* awareness, we can re-awaken the skills we were born with but outgrow, which is tuning in to the useful, enjoyable and sensual information that flows both around and through us (Box 6.1). It may seem too obvious to say as you sit in the cosy isolation of reading this, but groups are a densely complex piece of our world, every bit as weird, strange, conflicted, and obscure as the society that gives rise to them. Imperfect as they are, if we are willing to be awake to group processes rather than becoming seduced or subsumed by them, then we have a chance to learn not just about ourselves, but about others too. We may even begin to understand how the distractions and apparent cul-de-sacs in which a group flounders could indicate something deeper about what is going on in the meeting room, and beyond in the wider organisation.

Box 6.1 *A Gestalt Perspective*. Awareness in a group

NOW is of great importance to the gestalt perspective. What you notice at this moment in time is known as *foreground*. It encompasses what grabs your attention right now. In the same way that staring intensely at an object blots out its surroundings, so focusing solely on the foreground distracts us from its context. Western culture seduces us into seeing our senses as a less-powerful platform to understand the world, favouring instead our intellect alone. Allowing our senses to experience what ordinarily goes unnoticed takes us beyond foreground to *background*. The aim of the gestalt approach is to achieve a mutually satisfying experiential relationship with the self, others, and our environment by sensing foreground *and* background.

Exercises. If possible, try this next time you are in a meeting. Bring into awareness your breathing – notice the coolness of your breath as you inhale and its warmth as you exhale. Notice the scents around you, the aura of the room, natural odours and their substitutes, such as perfumes and aftershaves from the people around you. Can you describe what is happening in the group without needing to rationalise it? Listen as if you are about to reflect back what someone in the group says – it focuses your attention on the foreground. Then notice when you drift off into your daydreams, memories or imaginings; this is background. Do not force yourself to perform well at this. Perhaps narrate the process inwardly, saying to yourself: "now I am aware that …".

Listen with your body – do you notice tension in your chest, shoulders, hands, or back? How are you responding emotionally to what is being said? Do you feel bored, distracted, or irritated? Can you visualise these feelings as, say, helium balloons floating off into the sky? Have you noticed whether what somebody says is at odds with his or her non-verbal behaviour? Does what you feel correspond with what is happening in the room? Do you notice others communicating through behaviours (i.e. phone-checking, doodling, drumming fingers, staring at the wall, or at you)? Do you notice any shift in mood in the room? How do you experience silences?

Through increased awareness of foreground and background, you may begin to notice what you, others, and the group fears, feels angry about, or is avoiding. This is useful data for later in the chapter.

The purpose of this chapter is not to prepare you for working therapeutically with groups, or indeed to provide you with the skills for leading groups, although there are excellent resources available for this (see Houston, 1990; and Rogers, 2010). I want instead to share some perspectives myself and others have found useful for waking up to the powerful forces that emerge when we gather together to do something. Being aware of and not merely seduced by what groups do will give you a richer palette of choices about your role in and the potential outcomes of what happens when we work together.

The fluidity of boundaries and the importance of cohesion

No matter how ephemeral or fleeting a group or team is, it comes together to *do* something. So what is it that turns a collection of individuals into a group? How do we make sense of our shift in perspective from being an individual to becoming a member of a group? It is something that feels both effortless and yet elusive. You are walking down the high street, vaguely aware that there are half a dozen or so strangers around you: the girl walking her dog, the couple browsing in a shop window, and the man poised to cross the road nearby. You would not consider yourself a member of a group in that moment. Suddenly a man collapses a few metres away. You and those around you, I hope, respond through some kind of rudimentary concerted action to help the person in trouble. A group has formed. It has purpose and function. It may last for just a few minutes until an ambulance arrives or it may evolve over the years into a national scheme to ensure defibrillators are available in all public places.

Some of the most important questions we have about groups include: what holds us together? What triggers their fragmentation, and how do they respond to their environment? The effortless fluidity of these processes is readily illustrated using a metaphor based on my favourite form of transport. Picture several strangers pedalling along the road on their bicycles doing what looks like the same thing at the same time and possibly even in the same direction. Just like the previous scene on the high street, you would not consider this collection to be either a team or group. But if they do come together for the common purpose of minimising wind resistance and therefore fatigue they become a group – or *peloton*, in the case of cyclists. Once organised into a peloton something greater than the sum of the individual parts is created. The *peloton* adopts a set of assumptions about its purpose and goals that defines its *boundary*. It is what distinguishes the peloton from other road users and their environment.

We are reminded of attachment theory when we think about the group boundary, which defines order and security, and beyond which lies potential danger, insecurity, and unpredictability. Boundaries help balance our need to belong to something bigger than ourselves with the competing desire for solitude. Boundaries offer a defence against our fear and the anxiety of what is uncertain in our world. The oft-heard expression "that's above my pay grade", or "it's more than my job's worth" is a statement defining a boundary, protecting the speaker from unreasonable demands asked of them. Yet in defining our boundary, we also invite fear and anxiety because it may be challenged or attacked, for example with: "oh yes, it is your pay grade!" Boundaries are a source of safety *and* anxiety because they need to be patrolled, policed, and even defended. The compulsion to manage anxiety and uncertainty in organisations leads us to create silos, niches, or subgroups. We develop our own jargon, which leads to creeping isolation and ultimately atomisation as boundaries become barriers between people.

Everyone agrees that groups with a strong sense of cohesion are better able to defend themselves against internal and external threats. Yet it is a phenomenon that eludes a clear definition. When our *peloton* achieves a critical size, subgroups or teams emerge which engage in complex practices, both exploiting and supporting the existence of the group-as-a-whole (see Case Study: Box 6.7). As in all groups, members of the *peloton* are aware of experiencing shifts between their different roles and identities. Members are, of course, individuals with their own inner worlds of needs and wants (i.e. "I am hungry"). Individuals have relationships to others, both within (i.e. "I need to pick up food for my team mate") and beyond (i.e. "the rider in front of me is losing concentration and could cause a crash") their subgroup or team. And, of course, the individual is in relationship with the peloton as a *whole* (i.e. "we are speeding up because we have a tail wind"). Each member of the group must be able to switch between these relationships for the group-as-a-whole to survive, develop, and transform (Agazarian, 1999). The sum of these relationships, including that of the *peloton* or group-as-a-whole with its environment or landscape, contributes to the notion of group *cohesion*. A prevailing wind in an exposed landscape, for example, serves to submerge any internal competition between subgroups for the greater good of the *peloton*. Cohesion is what motivates individuals to exhaust themselves at the front of the *peloton* to ensure that the star climber of their subgroup is well positioned and relatively fresh for the big climb of the stage.

Members of cohesive groups try harder to influence other members, are more open to being influenced themselves, listen more carefully, are more accepting, are prepared to self-disclose, and experience greater levels of security and relief from tension (Yalom & Leszcz, 2005, p. 75). The fundamental role of a group, therefore, is having somewhere to belong. Rogers' deep insights into the *Relational Approach* are as relevant to group cohesion as they are to our dyadic relationships (see chapter 3 in Rogers, 1971). A cohesive group is a place to internalise our sense of order, an idea central to how therapeutic groups work. They afford a safe and secure environment where security is earned then internalised (Roisman *et al.*, 2002). Empathy, unconditional positive regard, and authenticity – characteristics of the *clan* culture – are all present in a cohesive group in sufficient amounts to counterforce the potentially dehumanising forces encountered at work.

Teams and attachment

Group attachment is a combination of both how we see ourselves in the group and how we see the group as a potential attachment figure. It is distinct from a one-to-one dynamic as the group provides a more public kind of reassurance, self-worth, and motivation (Smith *et al.*, 1999). People defaulting to an anxious attachment strategy in a group tend to keep problems to themselves to avoid either making trouble or triggering conflict. They may even hold negative views about themselves as members of the group (i.e. "nobody likes/notices me"), assuming that others will think the worst of them. Take Trudy, for example, who is running late for an important meeting. The situation triggers for her negative self-evaluations such as: "they think I'm incompetent ... I will be excluded". On arrival she becomes defensive and prickly in anticipation of being criticised or rebuked. Her anxious attachment strategy struggles to frame the group as an entity that could be accepting and trusting of its members. An alternative avoidant approach means playing fast and loose with boundaries such as time, confidentiality, and place. It may also involve being elusive and hard to pin down, or ignoring team members and not going to the trouble to socialise. Research demonstrates that such insecure attachment strategies adapt positively to the warmth and trust consistent with a *Relational Approach* (Roisman *et al.*, 2002). Our expectations of security can be built through the methodical modelling of non-judgemental acceptance, interpersonal honesty, and spontaneity. So when Trudy is greeted with authentic smiles and a "welcome" along with a genuine show of concern for her wellbeing, the chances are she will gradually learn that she need no longer arrive on the defensive, because an attack is not imminent.

The idea of team cohesion generally reflects a sense of trust and comfort among members. It is the belief that we can effectively resolve and survive its internal conflicts. Although working in a team with a range of attachment strategies in operation may not always feel enjoyable, they actually function quite well together (Lavy *et al.*, 2015). Because of the complex nature of team-working, a range of attachment orientations and therefore responses needs to be available to meet the challenges of different stages of what a team meets to achieve. Much like a sports team, tall or short, fast or powerful, there is a place for all because diversity means that the team is able to respond rapidly to new situations and opportunities. However, team diversity is not to be confused with Meredith Belbin's classic formulation of *team roles*, much beloved of management consultants and the like. Here, dubious conclusions drawn from experiments conducted in the 1970s on male-dominated, hierarchical, leader-centric bureaucracies suggests that effective teams rely on functions, and not on our qualities as human beings (see Box 6.2; Belbin, 1981).

Box 6.2 Belbin's team roles

What the roles bring, and the skills they offer

- *Plant* – creative, imaginative with problem-solving skills.
- *Resource investigator* – enthusiastic with good communication skills.
- *Coordinator* – mature, delegator and decision-maker.
- *Shaper* – dynamic and driven to act.
- *Monitor/evaluator* – sober judgement with evaluative skills.
- *Team-worker* – cooperative and socially skilled.
- *Implementer* – reliable and practical.
- *Completer* – conscientious and a finisher.
- *Specialist* – dedicated with relatively rare skills and knowledge

---

What we lose in the virtual group. Increasingly, much of our work is done in virtual environments which can be in *real-time* such as when we Skype and video conference, or *out-of-time* through emails and texts. Virtual meetings are now becoming as common as face-to-face ones as teams of people conduct collaborations across the globe without ever coming together in the same physical space. Because we are *not* being met as a *person* at work, we never become truly internalised by others, remaining a two-dimensional concept separated by a virtual divide. This invites many opportunities for miscommunication as our fantasies take over and fill in the gaps about who we really are as people. I can easily ignore the crackly interference of the virtual divide when I hear my favourite band on the radio having already internalised the experience of a live performance. In a similar way, without having met, you can be distorted by the virtual divide. It becomes harder to communicate our warmth, humour and humanity; we lose something essential about why we work. Yet virtual working is here to stay. A text conversation can feel as suffused with intimacy for some as a face-to-face conversation, even though it is devoid of old-fashioned stuff like eye contact. It seems non-intimacy is the new intimacy, and if we are to retain what is important about learning to trust, conveying empathy, and accepting each other, we will require creative approaches to being met as a person at work (Fletcher *et al.*, 2014).

The dark side of belonging – *ostracism*. As well as our own personal reservoir of self-esteem, we are often preoccupied with the evaluation of others in the groups to which we belong. As belonging is so fundamental, groups can be a potentially distressing source of rejection and exclusion as well as esteem. Ostracism is a painful attack on our sense of feeling significant and visible to others. It reminds us of what it might be like if we did not exist, a foretelling of our ultimate annihilation, with behavioural, emotional, and physical effects that can be both traumatising and long-lasting (Rotge *et al.*, 2014). Ostracism is easy to recognise and we have all experienced it to some degree. We have all felt the shame of being chosen last for a team game at school, or not invited to a party. As grown-ups, we can often feel distressed when we believe we have been excluded from a meeting, social get-together or even an email trail. Behaviours such as the denial of eye contact, a slight coolness in the tone of voice, avoidance or blanking someone as they pass on the corridor are mild indicators of the threat of ostracism. At the extreme level, criticism or outright shaming through ridicule also signal the risk of exclusion. Yet researchers consider ostracism to be a relatively normal and even an adaptive part of group processes because it controls difficult or deviating members through shame, and ironically increases cohesion and stability among those who do the rejecting (Williams, 2007). Ostracism in the workplace is costly for employers as it is linked with lower job satisfaction, higher turnover, and reduced psychological wellbeing (Wu *et al.*, 2016). Ostracism or indeed its threat is a form of emotional abuse and as such is an unacceptable means through which a group should modify so-called non-conformist behaviour, not just in the workplace, but beyond. We will return to ostracism and related forms of emotional abuse in Chapter 7, but some key ideas behind the *Dark Side* of groups are outlined in Box 6.3.

Box 6.3 The dark side of the group

Melanie Klein described the process of *splitting* as a way of denying aspects of ourselves that we find either destructive or unacceptable (Howard, 2010, pp. 108–115). *Projection* is how we further distance ourselves from our denied feelings by wrongly attributing them to others. Therefore, it is always worth asking: "*Is the person (or subgroup) being rejected by the group at some unconscious level being unfairly asked to carry a negative projection for everyone else?*"

Many of us will have encountered this when we blame or *scapegoat* other team members, those outside the team, or some depersonalised entity, i.e. "the union is kicking up a fuss", "HR will not like that", or "management are up to their usual tricks".

A team facing uncertainty about its future in the organisation may understandably feel hostile towards the system that has plunged it into crisis. A primitive response to this threat would be to *split-off* feelings of hostility and *project* them onto the least popular/likely to retaliate member of the team. The anxiety this provokes escalates out of proportion until the group becomes committed to rejecting the scapegoat as it thinks it must do so to survive. The target of scapegoating loses confidence and may even leave. The irony is that the anxiety remains, as the group learns what it can do to itself. Unless the cycle is intercepted, another scapegoat will have to be found to continue the displacement activity.

Containment is a way in which an individual (a supervisor, team leader, etc.) *holds* the anxiety of others, turning it into a set of alternative emotions that are less anxiety-provoking. It is a process of integrating then resolving *both* the good and bad of a group, through providing firm boundaries, i.e. guidelines, instructions, or use of authority, as distinct from being *authoritative*. The process is likened to a child feeling overwhelmed by the both the good and the bad in their parents. The capacity to simultaneously contain *both* comfortable and uncomfortable feelings is characteristic of Winnicott's "good enough" care-giver discussed in Chapter 5. The process of containment, which is about managing impulses rather than defending against them, can be usefully facilitated through effective mentoring or group supervision (Chapter 5; see also Thomas & Hynes, 2007).

The politically savvy operator. The fear of ostracism is a powerful motivator for those defaulting to an anxious attachment strategy. To defend themselves against the fear of rejection, the politically savvy operator creates their own group, which in its turn is dependent on *them*. Robert Caro's magisterial biography of Lyndon B. Johnson (1982) is an exquisitely detailed case study of the quintessential politically savvy operator who manipulated those around him right from school to the highest office. The politically savvy operator is perfectly adapted to slithering through the managerial bureaucracy, proving time and again that you do not have to be good to be great. They are often complex, visionary, contradictory, and opportunistic figures who thrive in hierarchical organisations. Gerald Ferris and colleagues (2007) characterise the politically savvy individual as someone who is adept at shaping, persuading, and manipulating others in their organisation. These successful influencers focus entirely on their own goals and in doing whatever helps to achieve them. They are finely attuned to their context, keenly empathic towards others, and remarkably self-aware with the capacity to be flexible and chameleon-like in how they present themselves to others. Importantly, the politically savvy operator can do all this and more so long as they can maintain the pretence of sincerity (see Box 6.4). I will return to the politically savvy operator and their role in emotional abuse later in Chapter 7.

Box 6.4 Characteristics of the politically savvy operator

Socially astute. They are affable, pleasant, attuned to diverse social settings, and accurate observers of others. They have the capacity to empathise and understand exactly what motivates *others*. Because these skills are *outward-facing*, politically savvy individuals are self-aware without being self-absorbed.

Interpersonally influential. Savvy people are flexible, unassuming, and have a convincing personal style that adapts and calibrates to different situations to get the desired responses from others. *Self-promotion* is a favoured tactic to appear competent: too little fails to impress, too much conveys arrogance or conceit. *Ingratiation* has the tactical intention of being liked by influential others. It can of course extend to the genuine praise of colleagues; yet strategic praise can be interpreted as manipulation.

Networking. Savvy people are adept at identifying and developing a diverse range of contacts across their organisations. They are able to develop friendships and strong, beneficial alliances and coalitions horizontally with peers, and more importantly vertically with power brokers for upward appeal.

> **Sincere.** If attempts to be influential are going to be successful, it is important to at least appear to have high levels of honesty, integrity, and authenticity. Insincere self-promotion simply comes across as doing whatever is necessary to get ahead, which may be problematic amongst peers, but only adds to upward appeal.

Emergent behaviours

More is different. Jobs in organisations during the early twentieth century were considered things apart from the people who were doing them. The emphasis then, and unfortunately remains for many organisations and researchers, on the scientifically informed selection of a person to fit a job (Chapter 2). This reductionist approach to people reflected the mood of the time, which sought to understand and manage complexity by defining the individual parts that compose the whole. The explanatory arrows point down in much the same way that they did in the natural sciences until Werner Heisenberg, in developing quantum mechanics at around the same time, drew our attention to the central role of uncertainty. The embarrassment of data collected during the Human Genome Project, for example, shows us that any enterprise that seeks to discover intricate patterns of causation in the dynamic and interactional complexity of living systems is ultimately doomed. Scientists at the Institute for Adaptive Matter are instead pioneering research into the role of emergent behaviour in the natural sciences, which simply put means "more *is* different". The principle of organic-*ism* understands that the behaviour of a living system is not attributable to its components, but instead arises through the relationship between the components, often transcending what any individual may intend, comprehend, or even perceive. We are by definition emergent beings, because the individual cells that come together to form a person do not contemplate their place within the whole. Even if it were possible to understand a person as an isolated entity, it would not be feasible to predict the behaviour of the group formed when many of us come together. For groups, emergence means behaviours that arise *through* the interaction of people, and not as a summation of individual relationships. A useful metaphor for group emergence is to see it as akin to the process of rain falling on still water; the asymmetries in the droplet size, velocities, and spacing creates patterns of splashes and waves that collide, interfere, merge, amplify, and coalesce in a manner beyond the ken of any individual droplet.

The earliest hint that emergent behaviours would undermine attempts to reduce complex human systems to their constituent cogs came from studies

Figure 6.1 Emergent Processes.

carried out in the 1920s and 1930s at the Hawthorne site of the Western Electric Company in the USA. A series of experiments in scientific management investigated how lighting levels and rest breaks, for example, influenced productivity. In the "illumination room" experiment, the lights for one group of workers were varied while those for the control were unchanged. An agreed explanation for why both groups increased their productivity eludes researchers to this day. The chief populariser of the studies at the time, Elton Mayo, explained this and other equally perplexing findings in terms of the *human factor*. He argued that because people in both groups felt they were of interest and importance to the researchers, their motivation to be productive increased. Capitalists had already suspected we were more complicated than cogs in a machine. English towns such as Port Sunlight and Bourneville have at their foundation the belief that we can optimise the productivity of the human resource by manipulating the environment where people live and work. In short, both the Scientific Management and Human Resource approaches seek to maximise productivity through either *avoiding* or *manipulating* human relationships.

Three identifiably different *scientific* approaches to understanding group behaviour evolved since the Hawthorne studies (Mathieu *et al.*, 2018). The *Harvard* school saw teams as self-contained social systems, with the individuals in them behaving as elements of a larger social system. The dominant *Michigan* school, initiated by the prominent social psychologist Kurt Lewin, advanced a much more individualistic approach. Here, a person's perception of their environment is seen as the guiding influence in their behaviour, which is understood through classical reductive scientific methods. Much like the atom in chemistry, the individual is seen as the "*lowest meaningful unit in the human social system*". Contemporary researchers reflect ruefully on how the assembly of teams based on an optimal mix of knowledge, skills and characteristics is rarely possible without "compensatory interventions" to correct for the human factor. The third *Illinois* school is an integration of ideas from both the Harvard and Michigan traditions, adopting a dual focus on individual members and the group-as-a-whole. During the past 25 years, organisational psychologists have focused more on the experience of the individual in teams and their cognitive processes in problem solving tasks. The team is seen as something like a static knot in an organisational net, with little or no interest in interpersonal skills, trust, or the collective emotions or moods of people (Kozlowski & Ilgen, 2006, p. 93).

Although there have been thousands of "scientific" studies on what makes teams effective, the deterministic approach will not help our understanding of such inherently unpredictable human systems. Excessive reductionism leads to the distorted idea that insight is gained only by looking *downwards* and *inwards*. Nobody doubts that details matter, but the organic-*ismic* view is grounded not in the internal structures of groups, but on what emerges from the relationships *between* people in groups.

Forming, storming ... and so on. You may already be familiar with Bruce Tuckman's model that proposes four stages of small group development, with a fifth stage of *mourning* tacked on later to take into account what happens towards the end (see Box 6.5). The catchy phrase captures the essence of most other stage models that are often criticised for being overly simplistic and linear in how they see an otherwise complex, emergent and unfolding process (Yalom & Leszcz, 2005, chapter 11).

In developing his model, Tuckman was reflecting on the experiences of people in therapeutic or other similarly *closed* groups, i.e. ones with clearly defined boundaries around membership and confidentiality. For this reason, we should be cautious when applying this model to the kind of *open* groups encountered in the workplace. Furthermore, the model only describes what happens in a group when left to its own devices. It does not follow that task-oriented workplace teams develop through similar linear stages with such easily recognisable characteristics. Unskilful interventions by a manager or disruptive behaviours by team members competing for prominence undermine a team's chances of ever achieving the performing stage. Harry Truman recognised the truth of this after skilfully guiding his monumental European Recovery Programme (*The Marshall Plan*) into existence in 1948, reflecting; "it was remarkable how much could be accomplished if you didn't care who received the credit" (McCullogh, 1992, p. 564). Notwithstanding these cautionary notes, Tuckman's model offers us an accessible language to begin a conversation about what happens in groups, and how to avoid becoming disoriented by the complex dynamics of group processes (Bonebright, 2010).

Box 6.5 Tuckman's stages of group development

Forming. This describes the period when a group becomes oriented to its environment, creates ground rules, and tests boundaries both relationally and with tasks. Anxiety about establishing ranking in the group is usually unspoken but present. As members begin to realise that solving problems as a group can be difficult, they may move to the next stage.

Storming. This is characterised by a lack of structure and conflict (i.e. anger, fear, and the shame of being exposed) as members compete for influence. Group members become hostile towards the facilitator and one another as a way of expressing their individuality, and as protest against losing themselves in the "crowd". The next phase can develop when this tension is resolved.

Norming. As consensual rules and boundaries are established, resistance is overcome and cohesion develops. The group emerges into something more than its parts. Work begins and conflicts are avoided to ensure harmony.

Performing. The final stage of the original model (1965) describes the group as a problem-solving instrument, as members adapt and play roles that will enhance activities. Energy is channelled appropriately, and something similar to the utopian group comes to the fore.

Mourning. Sometime after, Tuckman and Jensen (1977) recognised a fifth stage of development that reflected the life cycle of groups. As the ending of the group approaches, concerns turn to fear and anxiety around separation, disengagement, and endings.

Organisational rituals. Larry Hirschhorn (1988) coined this term to describe the most durable and observable forms of defence we have against what we fear at work. A *ritual* is something that can take on a life of its own, becoming disconnected from our rational experience. For example, it is common in the military for people to move around the organisation on tours of duty of up to two years at a time. Engineering in this level of interchangeability and depersonalisation makes perfect sense for teams working in hostile and hazardous environments; it purposefully undermines our attachment to people. However, this extreme form of atomisation creates chaos in terms of continuity and accountability, especially when working alongside civilians. Similarly, Isabel Menzies' ground-breaking study of a British hospital in 1960 identified how nursing professionals contained their own anxieties when working with the sick and dying by depersonalising their relationship with those they were caring for. Just like the military, a uniform enables us to become part of a faceless army, in this case, of interchangeable helpers. The fragmentation of care – for example, with one professional dealing with the drug round, and another doing all the bedpans – ensures that people do not become attached to each other. Someone's desperately ill husband, father, brother, or uncle becomes reduced to an acronym at the end of their bed, i.e. "DNR" (Do Not Resuscitate). Bureaucracies depersonalise to help us not think, and not thinking helps us feel less fearful and anxious (see *Functional Stupidity*, Chapter 2). Yet defences solve nothing, and only serve to help us short-circuit our fear and anxiety. In this way we are all prevented from thinking, reflecting, feeling, and learning at work. Take a moment and consider the rituals designed to help you not think in your organisation. Perhaps it involves an unquestioned allegiance to organisational rank, and "knowing your place" in the hierarchy? Next, we look at what psychoanalysis offers us by way of further insight into what I referred to earlier as our emotional PPE.

Basic assumptions. It was Wilfred Bion (1897–1979) who first introduced the idea that a level of unconscious collusion exists in groups that derails or subverts the rational and efficient work of what we meet to do. He coined the term *work group* to describe something approaching the utopian collective described earlier. Here, all members actively contribute, and those with appropriate competence are given the space to be involved in a way that does not relieve others from joining in, or importantly from accepting responsibility for themselves. The work group is open to new ideas, and conflict fuelled by our anger, fear, and shame can be examined safely and non-defensively; roles are distinguished from people so that what is said is not personalised. This state of perfection does not last long, if it exists at all, before we drift into feeling bored, begin bickering with each other, get angry, feel stuck, or start to go round in circles.

Bion noticed that at this point people appeared to behave *as if* they had gathered to do something else, perhaps because of a collective anxiety about what they had gathered to do in the first place. By adopting a *basic assumption*, the group finds a way to survive the crisis of anxiety, which in turn disrupts their productive work. He carefully chose the term *assumption* to emphasise his point that there appeared to be no apparent rational explanation for our behaviour other than it seemed to be based on some collective fantasy. Some argue that our *basic assumptions* reflect deeper, unspoken, and not necessarily conscious systems of thinking and feeling which mirror our earliest relationships (Moxnes, 1998). The *basic assumptions*, which I explore next, seem to bubble beneath the surface of all our groups, organisations, and wider cultural structures. They have at their core *helplessness* in the case of *dependency*, anger and fear in the case of *fight/flight*, and *fantastical hope* in the case of *pairing*.

Dependency. A group that flips into this basic assumption adopts the unofficial aim of searching for some idealised, omnipotent authority figure or its equivalent to rescue them. The group rejects its capacity for competence and creativity and instead appears more committed to identifying someone or something that can measure up to the fantasy of a God or monarch who will rescue their helpless subjects. Bion identified the *Church* as a good example of an organisation that mobilises and uses such a basic assumption. I find it intriguing, too, how having failed to effectively tax our planet's billionaires, we look to them instead to undertake transcendent global tasks such as eradicating diseases, halting climate change and even colonising the solar system on our behalf. On a more modest scale, those of us who work with groups as a facilitator, teacher, mentor, coach, supervisor, or when chairing a meeting, etc. will be familiar with the seductive and hopefully fleeting notion that we could be some kind of messianic saviour. Yet any attempt to live up to the expectations of the group in this regard is ultimately doomed, as nobody can possibly fulfil this role.

In failing to meet the expectations of the dependency fantasy, hostility, and perhaps even rejection by the group follows. Anxious trainees demand more and more from their trainer (e.g. handouts, PowerPoints, directed learning, reading lists, tutorials, video recordings of the session, etc.) but to no avail; in doing so, the facilitator only fuels the flames of helplessness. Group members may begin to view their leader as either incompetent or unable to see what is really going on within the group or organisation. An interesting manoeuvre by the group might be to identify a member (or subgroup) who needs the special attention of the leader, i.e. an especially anxious trainee. Here, the group is not so interested in supporting one of their own, but in signalling the group's dependency on their leader to rescue them.

What to do: Bringing into awareness the group's fantasy that it needs to be dependent will raise useful questions about what it hopes to achieve through this behaviour and who will profit from it. A group or team that can free itself from its fantasy of dependency can begin to claim its autonomy and creativity, rather than having a leader delegate it to them.

Fight or Flight. This basic assumption is about our fundamental sensitivity to some imaginary danger or threat, and the fantasy is that the group has met to preserve itself through either fighting or running away from something, rather than working together. The group behaves *as if* it is being attacked; paranoia and imagined enemies abound. Action becomes essential, and so the group fantasy demands a vigorous leader or manager (*the hero*) who can encounter and battle with enemies and dangers (*the villains*). The hero need not even identify a villain who is a real person, but can instead mobilise ideas such as: a shortage of time (we need to act quickly), reflexivity (we waste time consulting), structures (the system is against us), the economy (we have to tighten our belts), or even the fear of being left behind (we must change or become dinosaurs).

As the basic assumption takes hold, lawlessness ensues with a "survival of the fittest" narrative prevailing. Effective and professional people or teams become targets for vilification, and get incorrectly identified as being "over-resourced, lazy, over-staffed, or disengaged". I find that this basic assumption is at its most raw in the context of training counsellors and psychotherapists who use groups for the sole purpose of personal development, i.e. a group for experiencing being in a group. Classic avoidant behaviours such as arriving late or not at all, whispering, discussing neutral "safe" topics or trivia, and phone-checking, etc. all serve to block the anxiety-provoking work. You have either noticed, colluded with, or even been the silent communicator in a group setting. You know – the person who distracts others from the agenda or the reason for meeting, the non-participant who is busy with other activities such as texting, catching up with emails, staring out the window, or doodling.

What to do. Bringing into awareness a group's fantasies about needing to identify both a villain (the anxiety of personal development, say) and a hero (behaviours that rescue us from anxiety) raises potentially useful questions about what it achieves and who profits from this behaviour. Both the military and to some extent political movements cap-italise on the basic assumption of fight/flight, identifying fantasy villains such as "terror", "foreigners", or even an economic collective of European states.

Pairing. The basic assumption here is that the group, instead of coming together to confront and overcome a challenge through collaboration, meets instead to enable a partnership (their sex is largely irrelevant) and create something new that will rescue the group from anxiety. This could include another leader, some exciting initiative, or a solution to an old problem. Bion calls our attention to the emotional atmosphere that accompanies this basic assumption, especially hope and optimism that an old problem will disappear because some new, fantastical fusion will produce utopia.

We have all witnessed how the crisis of an apparently intractable problem is "solved" in a meeting by somewhat flirtatious promises of a post-meeting "catch-up" that either does not happen, or is quickly forgotten (see Box 6.6). Training groups and work teams that flip into this assumption can become the beguiled audience to a pair of its members engaging in a discussion that seeks to solve some problem on their behalf. Yet if a group operating under this basic assumption actually comes up with a new idea, solution, or leader, then the intoxicating and seductive notion of hope will be weakened as they soon realise there is now nothing new to hope for. Organisations whose purpose it is to create a better world may well be founded on such assumptions. The announcement of a new and exciting joint venture, initiative, or another underfunded and toothless watchdog to monitor the quality of our air/water/education/health, etc. generally promises renewed hope but instead only ends in despondency and low morale. We appear perpetually addicted as a culture to monarchies, for example, who seem to exist only to reproduce. They feed our insatiable desire for hope through their all too public cycle of engagements, weddings, births, baptisms, and so on.

Box 6.6 A crisis averted?

Heidi, who manages several teams, convenes a "crunch" meeting with a problem group. The purpose is to resolve blocks to her planning for the forthcoming business cycle. At the heart of the difficulty is an anxiety-provoking interpersonal clash between members of that particular team. After a period of agreeable yet avoidant discussions, Heidi moves to conclude the meeting by proposing that the team leader, along with one other nominated member of the group, come to her by the end of the week to present their solution to the crisis. During the course of the week, Heidi avoids responding to emails from the team leader who sought to confirm the meeting, which ultimately does not happen. Although the crisis has been averted, the problem remains unresolved.

Our world joins us when we join a group

What Bion observed in his practice as a group therapist must be seen in the context of his own relational biography and the times in which he lived and worked. The eight-year-old Bion was sent to boarding school and effectively abandoned by his parents. He recalls an unavailable, cold, frightening mother and an angry father, claiming in fact that he hated them both. Many years later as a therapist and group leader, he adopted an avoidant leadership style, choosing to say very little, thereby minimising his engagement with the group for fear of inviting "parental responsibilities". A group leader adopting this avoidant way of relating, as attachment theory would put it, certainly invites disproportionate levels of scrutiny about their role. Even though his ideas flourish as a method for understanding emerging processes in organisations, the stereotype of the inscrutable leader, in what is known as the Tavistock approach, is a world away from a *Relational Approach* and is largely abandoned as a technique for group therapy.

When transplanting Bion's thinking to our contemporary settings, it is worth remembering the implied *homogeneity* (i.e. white military men in post-war Britain) of the groups in which he worked and made his observations. It was perhaps not so obvious then that when joining a group, we bring the world in which we live along with us. The importance of the subgroups to which we already belong (i.e. unchosen characteristics such as race, sex, gender, age, ethnicity, and so on) gives us separate identities both within and across our groups. Whatever groups we join, we unquestionably already belong to identity groups first, in our own minds and in the eyes of others. Individual group members' anxieties about how the wider gaze of the group-as-a-whole will see them, interpret their feelings, promote their interests, and so on means that individuals rely on subgroups to provide an alternative setting where fear, shame, and even anger can be processed with confidence.

When working in groups or teams, it is vital that we hold in mind the subgroups to which we already belong. How might these subgroups help us form alliances, and how might these alliances enable or inhibit the completion of tasks we may wish to accomplish? While acknowledging that a group's development has some predictable features, Yvonne Agazarian recognised that the partial fragmentation of a group into subgroups was an important and potentially useful process (1999). Feeling different in a large group is, after all, an anxiety-provoking experience. There is a risk of being misunderstood or appearing too different. It feels much safer to talk about ourselves with others whom we feel we have more in common. We feel there is less chance of being shamed, judged, rejected, or bullied. Agazarian further emphasised the importance of supporting a group move through three phases that she identified as *authority*, *intimacy*, and *work* by paying attention to these subgroup processes.

Box 6.7 Agazarian's partial fragmentation in action

Working with subgroups in the context of psychoeducation

While working for the NHS I developed psycho-educational workshops for groups of couples affected by perinatal depression. To ensure the workshops were inclusive, the needs of subgroups (i.e. men, women, carers, and couples) were integrated alongside the following work tasks of *normalising, reframing*, and *reciprocity* (Costello, 2016).

Normalising. For men to manage the challenge to their self-esteem when encountering a perplexing problem such as perinatal depression, it seemed important to establish whether their problem was "normal". The process of normalising was best facilitated through sharing with others who were either experiencing or had encountered and survived something similar. This was achieved by working with subgroups of carers, who were often but not always men. As Harry explained: "*For me, it was about hearing that others go through it and survive … learning that I was not very different from others welcomed me back to the human race*".

Reframing what seems to be an external problem. Men were more likely to join the group believing that some *technical* problem lay with their partner, i.e. "you just take pills for it". A facilitated process of reframing gently challenged masculine assumptions, loosening the grip on ideals of autonomy and competence, enabling the process of emotional integration to begin. This was facilitated through couple subgroup and whole-group working. For example, I was volunteered to vocalise on behalf of the carer subgroup's (a role playfully called the "nominated bastard") fears and concerns that would otherwise have been intolerable in the risky environment of the group-as-a-whole. Reflecting on his role as a carer, one man recognised: "*Did I fail? Was I good enough to look after my wife? Maybe not … but I did succeed in seeing how I needed help*".

Reciprocity and indebtedness. Men are much more likely to seek help when they perceive there is also an opportunity to help others. Masculine ideals of strength and competence are preserved when we avoid feeling indebted. When a subgroup of carers are working together, they notice that they can empathise with others who are experiencing something similar. By revealing feelings that might be shaming in other settings, group cohesiveness increased. Carers become more available to offer their perspectives, share something of themselves, and support their peers and, ultimately, their partners.

The *authority phase* involves the basic assumption of flight and fight (fear/anger) during which the group may succumb to scapegoating. Subgroups represent an *intimate* container for conflict to be worked through, which gives time and space to the group-as-a-whole to learn how to integrate anger, shame, and fear. The purposeful use of functional subgroups is a practical way of containing conflict in the group-as-a-whole. The case study presented in Box 6.7 reflects how a subgroup (i.e. carers who are mainly men) who feel ashamed about expressing their feelings in the risky gaze of the group-as-a-whole (which contains their partners) are supported in a more intimate, homogeneous setting. By drawing on the experience of subgroups, integration of anxiety happens at three levels: the group-as-a-whole, the subgroup, and as individuals. Practically speaking, the process involves moving between various subgroups (i.e. for normalising and checking whether my experience is common), dyads (i.e. where couples engage in informal mentoring, where reciprocity, reframing, and sharing best practice takes place), and the group-as-a-whole process (resolving and integrating anxiety and potential conflict). Survival of the authority phase invites the transition to *intimacy* where idealisation, over-valuation, and enchantment invite closeness among members. Finally, the real *work* can begin as the group's sense of enchantment flips to a more realistic integration of how people, groups and organisations can be *both* good and bad, which reflects more accurately life itself.

Things to keep in mind

- Groups and teams are complex dynamic systems grounded on what emerges from the relationships between us.
- When in a group, begin noticing how you move between the *foreground* (i.e. your relationship with individuals) and the *background* we generally ignore, i.e. relationships with subgroups *and* the group-as-a-whole.
- Group cohesion is fundamental to healthy work teams. It is built on a *Relational Approach*, and involves a methodical modelling of non-judgemental acceptance, interpersonal honesty, and spontaneity.
- Emergent processes are how we manage the uncomfortable emotions of fear, anger, and shame. They prevent us from thinking and feeling, and solve nothing.
  - A team that can free itself from its fantasy of dependency claims its *autonomy and creativity*.
  - Challenging a team's fantasy that it needs to find both a villain and a hero raises important questions about what this behaviour achieves and who profits from it.
  - Noticing a team beguiled by a partnership that promises a new solution raises questions about what we are *avoiding*.
- Pay attention to subgroups. They are the foundation of alliances, which can support the healthy functioning of a team or group in the workplace.

References

Agazarian YM. (1999). Phases of development in the systems-centred psychotherapy group. *Small Group Research*, 30(1), 82–107.

Belbin RM. (1981). *Management teams: Why they succeed or fail.* Oxford: Butterworth-Heinemann.

Bonebright DA. (2010). 40 years of storming: a historical review of Tuckman's model of small group development. *Human Resource Development International*, 13(1), 111–120.

Caro, RA. (1982). *The years of Lyndon Johnson: The path to power.* New York: Alfred A Knopf Inc.

Costello JF. (2016). Men and perinatal depression. *Therapy Today*, 27(2), 14–17.

Ferris GR, Treadway DC, Perrewé PL, Brouer RL, Douglas C, & Lux S. (2007). Political skill in organizations. *Journal of Management*, 33(3), 290–320.

Fletcher KL, Comer SD, & Dunlap A. (2014). Getting connected: The virtual holding environment. *Psychoanalytic Social Work*, 21(1–2), 90–106.

Hirschhorn L. (1988). *The workplace within: Psychodynamics of organisational life.* Cambridge, MA: MIT Press.

Houston G. (1990). *The red book of groups.* Gillingham: Rochester Foundation.

Howard S. (2010). *Skills in psychodynamic counselling and psychotherapy.* London: Sage.

Kozlowski SWJ & Ilgen DR. (2006). Enhancing the effectiveness of work groups and teams. *Psychological Science in the Public Interest*, 7(3), 77–124.

Lavy S, Bareli Y, & Ein-Dor T. (2015). The effects of attachment heterogeneity and team cohesion on team functioning. *Small Group Research*, 46(1) 27–49.

Lee MY & Edmondson AC. (2017). Self-managing organisations: Exploring the limits of less-hierarchical organizing. *Research in Organizational Behaviour*, 37, 35–58.

Mathieu JE, Wolfson MA, & Park S. (2018). The evolution of work team research since Hawthorne. *American Psychologist*, 73(4), 308–321.

McCullogh D. (1992). *Truman.* New York: Simon & Schuster.

Menzies IEP. (1960). A case study in the functioning of a social system as a defence against anxiety. *Human Relations*, 13, 95–121.

Moxnes P. (1998). Fantasies and fairy tales in groups and organizations: Bion's basic assumptions and the deep roles. *European Journal of Work and Organizational Psychology*, 7(3), 283–298.

Rogers C. (1971). My way of facilitating a group. *American Journal of Nursing*, 71(2), 275–279.

Rogers J. (2010). *Facilitating groups.* Maidenhead: Open University Press.

Roisman GL, Padron E, Sroufe LA, & Egeland B. (2002). Earned-secure attachment status in retrospect and prospect. *Child Development*, 73(4), 1204–1219.

Rotge JY, Lemogne C, Hinfray S, Huguet P, Grynszpan O, Tartour E, George N, & Fossati P. (2014). A meta-analysis of the anterior cingulate contribution to social pain. *Social Cognitive and Affective Neuroscience*, 10, 19–27.

Smith ER, Murphy J, & Coats S. (1999). Attachment to groups: Theory and measurement. *Journal of Personality and Social Psychology*, 77(1), 94–110.

Thomas M & Hynes C. (2007). The darker side of groups. *Journal of Nursing Management*, 15, 375–385.

Tuckman BW & Jensen MAC. (1977). Stages of small-group development revisited. *Group and Organization Studies*, 2(4), 419–427.

Williams KD. (2007). Ostracism. *Annual Review of Psychology*, 58, 425–452.

Wu C-H, Liu J, Kwan H-K, & Lee C. (2016). Why and when workplace ostracism inhibits organizational citizenship behaviors: An organizational identification perspective. *Journal of Applied Psychology*, 101(3), 362–378.

Yalom ID & Leszcz M. (2005). *The theory and practice of group psychotherapy* (5th ed.). New York: Basic Books.

Chapter 7

The shadow at work

Relational abuse

The problem with defining bullying. Workplace bullying is a frightening, shaming, and sometimes life-shattering experience for those who go through it. My personal experience is reflected in what the research community finds, which is that it appears endemic in our organisations; this ought to trouble us all (Nielsen & Einarsen, 2018). Bystanders to bullying are not immune to its effects either. After all, what does it say about me as a human being if I can stand idly by and witness emotional vandalism without speaking up? Confusion begins the moment we start talking about "bullying". Are we referring to a set of clearly identifiable, emotionally abusive social behaviours (see Box 7.1), or alternatively, describing a purely subjective experience? The often banal nature of emotional abuse means that it is difficult to identify when it begins to happen and even harder to accept when it is going on. It often requires a concerned colleague to name the behaviour or the feelings it evokes before we can bring ourselves to either admit or recognise the experience for what it is. Although an imbalance of relational power is commonly implicated in the bullying dynamic, it is not always so clear-cut. We will return to the role of power in all its forms, including its abuse, later in this chapter.

Our reluctance to label a distressing experience with the term "bullying" is exacerbated by the associations attached to a word such as *victim*. In our Western patriarchal culture, it has uncomfortable connotations associated with being a loser, helpless, a precipitant, or even worse, a participant in this grim experience. In acknowledging, never mind reporting, our *victim* status we run the risk of shame and devaluation, either by ourselves or by others. Researchers point out that although both men and women are affected by psychological abuse in its broadest sense, it is not necessarily a gender-neutral phenomenon (Salin & Hoel, 2013). Masculine ideals of autonomy and competence are challenged by the implication of victimhood, meaning that men in particular are less likely to seek help when they feel targeted by abusive behaviours. It is not so black and white, however, and I have encountered and supported both men and

Figure 7.1 The shadow at work.

women who have felt shamed by their belief that they could not "handle the situation" on their own. I believe this is one of those issues where changing our language will genuinely help us speak more freely about the experience of bullying. Therefore, I want to promote the more neutral term *target* to describe a person or group of people who are or have been the object of psychological aggression. I will also use the term *perpetrator* to describe the person or group who, knowingly or otherwise, do the bullying.

Box 7.1 Behaviours usually associated with the term *bullying*

- Ridiculing or insulting someone, especially on the grounds of their sex, gender reassignment, race/ethnic/national origin, disability, religion, belief, sexual orientation, or age.
- Spreading rumours or insulting someone by word or behaviour.
- Ostracising someone or excluding them from group activities. Conversely, coercing someone into taking part in unwanted activities through fear of being ostracised.
- Setting someone up to fail, for example by giving them unrealistic targets or deadlines to meet. Unduly criticising their performance – especially publicly.
- Publicly undermining someone's authority.
- Overbearing supervision or other misuse of power or position.
- Making threats or comments about job security without foundation.
- Deliberately undermining a competent worker by overloading them or through constant criticism.
- Preventing an individual progressing by intentionally blocking promotion or training opportunities.
- Pressurising someone into not making a complaint, or labelling someone who has made a complaint of bullying or harassment as a "troublemaker".
- Unwelcome sexual attention – including sexualised banter.

Employee misbehaviour, bullying, gaslighting, harassment, incivility, mobbing, scapegoating, ostracism, passive aggression, victimization, and so on are all labels used interchangeably to describe emotional aggression. Some insist that the study of emotional aggression in the workplace is hindered by the plethora of labels used to describe it. From what I have witnessed, read, and experienced, I believe this to be the case. Yet sticking to specific terms can capture meaningful differences between, say, a single upsetting encounter with a peer to more persistent or ongoing emotional maltreatment over time. Bullying and harassment in particular are terms often used interchangeably, with the latter defined in law as: "*unwanted conduct related to a relevant protected characteristic, which has the purpose or effect of violating an individual's dignity or creating an intimidating, hostile, degrading, humiliating or offensive environment for that individual*" [EU Equal Treatment Directive (2006), UK Equality Act 2010, s26 2018].

Clear definitions of the term "bullying" remain elusive, not least of all because, as I explain later, it is contested like a football by the opposing teams of employer and employee. The important point is that whoever gets control of the ball – and employers have the home advantage – also get to dictate the rules of the game. To add to the confusion, there are many familiar euphemisms used to distract us from, disguise, or even excuse bullying in the workplace. In Box 7.2, I indicate some of the talk commonly used about perpetrators and targets: we must be alert to the former and sceptical about the latter when we encounter it in the workplace.

Box 7.2 Euphemisms which must alert us to emotional abuse

About the perpetrator

- A forceful, strong, straight-talking, or robust personality.
- Has an unfortunate manner.
- Does not suffer fools gladly.
- Not a people-person.
- A hard taskmaster, old school, or runs a tight ship.

About the target

- Overly sensitive.
- Can't take a joke.
- One of life's natural victims.
- A bit of a loner.
- Not a team player, a bit of a maverick, or is an outsider.
- Has an attitude problem or is a trouble-maker.

The hierarchy of emotional aggression. What most can agree on is that the overlapping terms in Box 7.1 are facets of the same thing, namely *emotional aggression*. The dynamic and nested array of interactions between organisational, subgroup, and interpersonal relationships can be viewed through the lens of a continuum of phenomena. Broadly speaking, assumptions and behaviours relating to emotional abuse tend to blend and merge with each other (Figure 7.2). The *meta*-level or overarching cultural assumptions and attitudes that I refer to as the *Corruption Complex* create the environment or climate for all psychological aggression to take place. The corruption complex draws our attention to the unquestioned assumptions that normalise competitive and abusive practices that influence what we do, what we are willing to tolerate, and what we assume we can get away with. For example, the *politically savvy* person understands that if you keep the little rules, you can break the big ones. If we are serious about addressing workplace misbehaviour, then we must address the broader structural and cultural assumptions that allow emotional aggression in organisations to be rewarded (Lutgen-Sandvik *et al.*, 2007).

Organisations invest a good deal of effort seducing us into believing that psychological aggression is readily reduced to a series of isolated interpersonal conflicts or spats. Such intermediate or *meso* behaviours refer to the more general forms of relational misbehaviour that are quite similar to each other, such as bullying and harassment. Specific workplace abuses now include illegal forms of discrimination around protected characteristics such as age, race, disability, etc. In practice, the experience of *meso* and certain *micro*-level types of abuse overlap. That is to say, sexual harassment can often cover behaviours that are not explicitly sexual or gendered, and yet at times bullying behaviour can be gender-based. Finally, highly personalised *micro* behaviours refer to things such as victimisation, incivility, and verbal hostility. Bullying and harassment, which can be seen as *meso* behaviours, include acts of incivility, passive aggression, ostracism, and scapegoating. What is important to acknowledge is that emotional aggression is done to us through relationships, so I will also use the term *relational abuse* to remind ourselves how central the interpersonal is to our wellbeing. We will explore this continuum of relational abuse in the following sections.

Figure 7.2 The hierarchy of relational abuse.

What fuels relational abuse? Before I go on to explore the hierarchy of emotional aggression, I want to emphasise how relational abuse must not be seen as just the act of some errant rogue, but as something that emerges through multi-layered and interconnected phenomena. In earlier chapters I explained how the big three emotions of anger, fear, and shame, ordinarily used to help us avoid danger, lie at the heart of our maltreatment of others in the workplace. Hierarchical and competitive market cultures that flourish in neoliberal economies confer hypernormal rules and expectations about *power*, *aggression*, and *competitiveness*: we accept them unquestioningly as the most sensible way to organise things. Bureaucracies seem the most obvious solution in a world where we no longer trust one other. In return for the apparent security conferred by this arrangement, we allow ourselves to be dehumanised, instrumentalised, and objectified. It is in the yawning gaps of our psychological contracts with each other that we experience anger, fear, and shame. Rarely is it made explicit that *we alone* must do the heavy lifting of emotional labour. Having to surface act, or be "grown-up" when working with those who abuse us, drives us into an unsustainable pantomime of inauthenticity. Our emotional biographies shape our *here-and-now* attitudes towards others, and draw us unthinkingly into the pernicious psychodrama of *Persecutor*, *Rescuer*, and *Victim* roles.

In groups and organisations, fear, shame, and anger are painful facts, and our defences against what can feel like unmanageable feelings solve nothing and only prevent us from thinking, feeling, and learning. Our capacity to *scapegoat* and *ostracise* lurk in the shadow of all groups, teams, and organisations. To manage the destructive manifestations of anger, fear, and shame we mistakenly project them onto individuals or others outside the group. What characterises the targets of scapegoating and ostracism is that they are either less powerful or less likely to defend themselves against their perpetrators. The fear of ostracism and rejection in such a hostile environment creates the conditions for the *political savvy* operator to flourish. These successful influencers are dedicated to the goal of manipulating and inveigling others into their own cabal or microcorruption complexes, where such practices are shown to pay off. It is in this context that I justified ethical supervision and compassionate mentoring as a safeguard against the exploitation of others as we work towards a more egalitarian working environment.

The corruption complex

The problem with seeing corruption from a narrow legal perspective is that it limits our understanding of misbehaviour at work. If we see corruption as simply describing those things clearly defined in law such as bribery, fraud, embezzlement, and extortion, then we fail to put a name to those other things that we know through experience to be wrong and unethical. Corruption at work is instead more usefully understood as the misuse of authority or power for personal gain, or for the benefit of some private clique to which a person or group of people belong. In action, this covers any breach of trust or unethical violation of formal workplace rules or policies by an employee entrusted with such powers in the course of doing their job. The point I want to make is: *behaviour can be both legal and corrupt*. This complex, nuanced, and socially intertwined relationship between improper and unethical practices has been termed the *corruption complex* by the anthropologist Jean-Pierre Olivier de Sardan (1999), and involves things like (Vickers, 2014):

Nepotism. This has to be top of the list of issues that actively undermine worker moral and trust in any hierarchy. The misuse of power around hiring people, or the award of status or promotion especially if it involves some financial benefit, is widely acknowledged as misconduct. *Homosocialisation*, introduced in Chapter 2, is rendered banal by euphemisms like "growing our own wood", a phrase used to justify giving jobs or positions to a favoured "good bloke/mate" or "one of us". Sophisticated organisations mask such inappropriate interference, especially for internal selection and appointment processes, by carefully constructing job specifications/business cases to fit the favoured. It is corrupt, and ironically constitutes a departure from the fundamental internal logic of the hierarchical bureaucracy, which is to depersonalise the workplace to reduce cronyism (Chapter 2). Willing accomplices or bystanders to what I would call, at best, maladministration hope that their compliance is rewarded in future competitions for positions of increased prestige, power, or authority. So must we endure the corruption complex to benefit from it? Unfortunately, it does not work like that, does it? In the longer run, standing by and doing nothing about nepotism only rewards such disingenuous conduct, and emboldens the reach of the informal alliances that already exploit us.

Influence peddling. The idea of insider trading need not be limited to the obviously illegal use of information about the stocks and securities of a public company. It can be extended to members of an organisation with access to privileged information who are willing to breach the trust invested in them by sharing it for the material gain of themselves, other individuals, or favoured networks. It is devilishly difficult to show unambiguously that "insiders" have already made their decisions about the outcome of quasi-transparent processes. A banal example could be a Hospital Trust that finds itself with a modest windfall to support some research, but the cash needs to be allocated quickly, through internal competition. A senior consultant on the research panel learns of this upcoming competition and alerts members of her favoured team, giving them the euphemistic "heads-up" for the forthcoming competition. The act of gifting a network with a distinctly unfair advantage is hard to prove, and grateful recipients make poor whistle-blowers.

Prevarication. Without actually resorting to an outright lie, we can manipulate the truth by being evasive, vague, deviating from, or even delaying giving others the information they need to do their jobs. So-called *inactive occupation* is about being starved of information or being excluded from the loop of communication, which includes information, emails, meetings, and so on. There are many subtle ways in which prevarication is used to deflect challenges to the questionable use of influence, position, or information in organizational life. Despite its subtlety, inactive occupation can be as emotionally damaging as other more direct and visibly aggressive behaviours. At its most banal, it means obfuscation (i.e. using jargon, and obscure or unclear systems of communicating information), deflecting direct questions, ignoring emails, or responding to them only after a request for information has ceased to be relevant.

Misuse of organisational resources. Information is power and nowhere is this truer than in the workplace. When withheld, changed, adulterated, manipulated, or misdirected then it constitutes corruption. Consider the example of a manager who manipulates work schedules or rosters to disadvantage others, or disrupt annual leave calendars in a way that makes it difficult for colleagues to plan their time. This behaviour increases anxiety and impacts negatively on workers' health and wellbeing. Misusing people's energy and time – often claimed to be the most valuable resource in an organisation – is a common source of frustration for any worker who has sat in a meeting and calculated how much staff time was being wasted assuaging a manager's anxiety about their status or authority. Limiting people to do work that is meaningless, demeaning or below their level of competence and skill leads to a loss of motivation or "rust-out". Here, a target's career progression, professional development, and confidence can be undermined at the same time as being removed from the gaze of influential others who might be able to support their progression. At the other end of the spectrum, burn-out is characterised by setting unreasonable deadlines or workloads which sets people up to fail. At a fundamental level both rust-out and burn-out constitute a serious misuse of organisational resources, compounded and legitimized by the use of policies such as performance management. Ironically, such punitive processes are often instigated by and, more worryingly, oblivious to the role played by the very manager who precipitates the crisis for a worker.

At an individual level it feels hard, if not impossible, to challenge behaviours that seem institutionally sanctioned and deeply embedded in the fabric of "how things have always been done around here", i.e. they are hypernormal. Are you sceptical about my belief that the corruption complex is an inherent aspect of your organisation? Would you dismiss me, saying: "it's all in your head, mate"? In the next part I explore why I think it is interesting you might even suggest that.

Am I mad or is this really happening to me?

The subjective experience. An employee approached his supervisor and asked her to reconsider the work roster: "I've been doing the graveyard shift for three years now, would you mind swapping shifts with me – it's only fair?" The supervisor responds: "I won't swap ... because avoiding the graveyard shift is a perk of being supervisor". The supervisor may genuinely believe that manipulating the roster is a time-served privilege that she has earned. It was, after all, how she was treated on joining the company. On the other hand, the subordinate sees his boss's pay as the earned privilege of her position, viewing her behaviour as an abuse of power. The feeling: "I am being exploited" forms the core of his subjective experience. *Feeling maltreated is legitimate even if the perpetrator fails to see or understand the impact of their actions.*

I once found it hard to believe how two people in the same relationship could see things *so* differently until I experienced it at first hand. As a psychotherapist in a staff counselling service, I became aware, only at the conclusion of the work, that I had been seeing both the target and the perpetrator of a bullying dyad. How they saw each other was so detached from my experience of them that it took a long time to put the pieces together. The target's life was rendered miserable by the perpetrator, and I supported her in wrestling with the pain and injustice of being emotionally abused. The perpetrator, on the other hand, was utterly blind to the impact she was having on those around her until she finally began exploring her own childhood experience of being casually ostracised by a socially powerful peer. What I learnt from this experience was that spending time trying to establish whether a perpetrator knowingly sets out to cause harm only shifts attention away from their behaviour and onto searching for potentially well-defended blind spots that may never enjoy the illuminating spotlight of self-awareness.

Psychological maltreatment cannot be measured by the extent to which a target experiences serious psychological symptoms, although as we see next, confusion, disorientation, and disbelief can form the core of the abusive relationship. It is also not about power imbalances, or a target being unable to defend themselves. Peer-to-peer and so-called upward emotional manipulation can be as real and every bit as disorientating as the sort of bullying classically encountered in the school playground.

In line with sexual or physical abuse, the behaviour of the perpetrator remains both *real and wrong*, irrespective of the power relationship, their level of self awareness or the subjective experience of the target.

Gaslighting. The 1930s play *Gas Light* is possibly the first artistic depiction of a form of emotional abuse that induces a person to doubt the validity of their own emotions, perceptions, thoughts, and beliefs in a way that ultimately undermines their sense of self-confidence (Burrow, 2005). In the MGM film of the same name, Charles Boyer plays Gregory, an emotionally abusive man who systematically and purposefully seeks to convince his wife Paula (Ingrid

Bergman) that she is losing her marbles by slowly chipping away at her self-belief. *Gaslighting* in its colloquial sense differs from the emotional manipulation perpetrated in the movie because it is not so goal-oriented, which in the case of Gregory meant getting his hands on Paula's jewels (Abramson, 2014). Nevertheless, the language and tactics employed by Gregory are both chillingly and accurately observed. The behaviours in the drama are initially characterised by social manipulations that isolate Paula from her affirming networks. They remove her from the gaze of those who can bear witness to the abuse and potentially intervene. The work of slowly undermining her sense of competence both with regard to herself, and to others begins: "you are prone to losing things ... I've noticed that you have been forgetful recently Paula ....".

The tactic of gaslighting often requires the participation of others who are either less able or unwilling to challenge the perpetrator's actions. Gregory inveigles the subordinate figure of the maid Nancy in the project of gradually undermining Paula's self-confidence. Emboldened by Gregory, Nancy even participates in excessive monitoring and characteristically hard to pin down behaviours towards Paula. Shame plays a key part in the way the *gaslighter* undermines their target's emotional world. For instance, when Paula explains to Gregory: "Nancy despises me", he immediately dismisses her emotional capacity, with "you are imagining things ... *like a silly child*". The gaslighter often uses diversion as a tactic to shift attention away from their target's emotions, focusing instead on their legitimacy as a moral agent or deliberator on how they see the world (Box 7.3). Fortunately (spoiler alert!), it is a fictional Mr Cameron who notices the signs of emotional abuse and supports Paula in challenging and ultimately escaping her tormentor.

Box 7.3 Tell-tale phrases used by the gaslighter

- Don't be so ... sensitive/paranoid/a prude
- You have no sense of humour
- You're overreacting, or just worked up
- It's just locker-room talk
- The same thing happens everywhere else
- It's all in your head ...
- Well ... that's only your interpretation/opinion

Gaslighting is about more than just being mistaken or wrong – it is about becoming convinced that I am in no fit state to make a judgement, as if it is all my fault. By accepting the gaslighter's interpretation of our subjective experience, we begin to mistrust our own emotions, which is why the targets of bullying often reflect: "I couldn't believe it was happening – even when it was *actually* happening". When something does not feel right, talk to someone you trust, get help and triangulate your experience (Box 7.4).

Box 7.4 Triangulate your experience

Gaslighting can feel disorientating and confusing when your sense of identity and capacity to believe in how you experience relationships is undermined. The seriousness of emotional coercion and control, especially through intimate familial relationships where we ordinarily expect to experience high levels of trust, is reflected by its criminalisation in the UK in 2015 (s76: Serious Crime Act).

When in doubt, speak to a trusted colleague, a union presentative, someone in HR, or perhaps all three. Triangulate perspectives; avoid becoming isolated in your experience, and get help.

What fuels the gaslight at work? The gaslighter's attitude to the emotional world of another person is the very antithesis of what characterises a *Relational Approach*. What is so despicable about gaslighting, I feel, is that a healthy perspective on reality and otherwise buoyant self-esteem, developed *through* trusting relationships, is undermined and unravelled *through* the abuse of trust.

So what lies behind gaslighting? It can take place against a background of power inequality, for example in market-oriented hierarchies that exists as a proxy for trust itself. When challenges to the prevailing narrative or power structure cannot be tolerated, the gaslighter goes on the offensive and seeks to manage their own anxiety by manipulating how you see their world (see Basic Assumptions, Chapter 6). In the context of holding onto your job or staying in the running for a promotion, it might feel easier to tell ourselves: "*perhaps* I am being too sensitive; *maybe* I do take things too seriously; I am *probably* being paranoid about this", and allow ourselves to be *gaslighted*. We do the emotional labour that Arlie Hochschild speaks of, and submit to the belief that speaking to power is the reserve of the privileged, and that only the rich can afford to put ethics before food on the table.

The Panopticon: How relational abuse maintains order

Benign abbot or menacing prison guard? It is difficult to understand what lies beneath the *corruption complex* at work without first considering the subtle and covert nature of power. I am not thinking about our more traditional understanding of power as discussed at the beginning of Chapter 5, which

Figure 7.3 The Panopticon.

is positional authority emanating from a suited boss behind a desk. Michel Foucault instead saw power as something less obvious and visible, something harder to grasp which resembles an invisible force dispersed throughout our social networks (1977). He saw how the soft disciplinary methods used for control in the workplace are reminiscent of the way monasteries have been organised for centuries. Indeed, the daily schedule in many organisations still mirrors the *divine offices* of monastic life. It begins around eight, with lunch at midday, and ends at around half five in the afternoon (i.e. *terce*, *sext*, and *vespers*, respectively). Having spent time in a monastic community, I understand how such structure, with its routines and hierarchy under the benevolent gaze of the abbot, invites the weary pilgrim into a soothed sense of detachment from thinking and feeling, for a time at least. In much the same way, we who submit to hierarchical systems also fall under the watchful gaze of the organisation, which subjects us all to constant observation, domination, and control.

We undergo a personal bureaucratisation when we enter an organisation. Your organisational identity, by which I mean your personnel files, appraisals, contract of employment, and the masses of ancillary policy and procedural documents to which you are subject, could fill a small room. This level of monitoring and measurement maximises the efficiency through which the organisation can utilise you. Reduced to a single individual case, out of context and atomised, it is easier for us to be judged, measured, and compared with one another. We also become vulnerable to the kind of emotional abuse that goes beyond "face-to-face" interactions. Through email/telephone response times, time sheets, innumerable key performance indicators (KPIs) and automated methods of supervision including computer recordings of downtime, we can feel like we are constantly being watched. How often do we hear of colleagues talking about "keeping their heads below the parapet", or "flying beneath the radar"? Our capacity to trust becomes something we outsource to a system of surveillance, and all we need do to remain acceptable to the organisation is to comply with those systems.

Foucault likened this organisational architecture of surveillance, or perpetual visibility, to the central viewing tower or *panopticon* of a prison complex. This angular architectural contraption represents the disciplinary drive exercised by the gaze of authority; observing, monitoring, and ultimately creating "docile bodies" – the stuff of a compliant society. In prison it is the gaze, or the threat of surveillance and not the surveillance itself, that disciplines. The watchful eye extends beyond the prison, which represents the panopticon in its purest form. Foucault invites us to pause and think about how prisons resemble factories, barracks, schools, and hospitals, which in their turn all resemble prison. This web of discipline is required by a technical society to produce compliant, industrious, conscience-ridden, useful creatures amenable to the modern tactics of production and warfare.

Understanding authority in this way, as an invisible yet pervasive force, has parallels with how electricity moves through a conductive material. All is well until some resistance to authority is met. In bureaucracies, the tension between worker resistance and compliance is encountered in the context of performance management, quality control, adherence to output KPIs, benchmarking, and so on. When resistance is strong, forces are mobilised to respond to and overcome the non-compliant worker (Hutchinson *et al.*, 2006). The worker who challenges the normal flow of power and authority becomes pathologised, and labelled the "problem". Middle managers collude in perpetrating organisationally sanctioned emotional abuse via "firm management", undermining worker collectives, or other tactics (Box 8.5). Bullying, whether it be conscious and rational or spontaneous and improvised, tends to be tolerated if it serves the broader interests of the organisation. In this way, bullying can be used strategically as a tool to maintain order alongside the coercive methods outlined earlier in Chapter 5.

In sophisticated organisations, overt bullying remains the nuclear option at the frontier of control. As a workplace counsellor, I have heard incongruent middle managers explain how they felt drawn into complex, vertical relationships, using terms like *grooming*, to describe how they were encouraged to nurture a *tough* reputation: "I made a pregnant woman redundant … they know I'm ruthless at the top … it's good for my career". Senior HR professionals who may have initial sympathy for targets of bullying ultimately close ranks and collude with the perpetrator: Ah yes … Stan can be *straight talking* … can't he? In non-unionised workplaces, or to a lesser extent in organisations with less than 100% union membership, it is the vulnerable worker, or those not in a union, who become easy targets for the serial perpetrators of emotional aggression (Pollert & Charlwood, 2009).

What big ears you have grandma! *All the better to hear you with … my dear.* It is important we recognise that organisational anti-bullying policies take a great deal of care to define what *is* and what is *not* bullying. In the way Little Red Riding Hood's granny was not as wholesome as she appeared, so the apparently worthy mission of an organisation in this respect has its shadow side (Liefooghe & Mackenzie Davey, 2010). We take it for granted that bullying is unsanctioned, interpersonal, and an abuse of individual power. An endemic organisational phenomenon is conveniently reduced to the misbehaviour of a few errant individuals. By reducing bullying to something that only happens to individuals, organisations are better able to position themselves as the *Rescuers* of hapless *Victims* such as you and me who live in fear of marauding bullies. The narrative distracts us from seeing the organisation as bullying through its own informally sanctioned practices and policies. Writing and then policing its invariably laconic anti-bullying policy means that the organisation reserves the right to choose its own line between the legitimate exercise of management power and any loosely interpreted statutory requirements in law. Blaming "bad apples" removes the need to look beyond systemic causes. Organisational representatives would rather pour resources into a high-value serial perpetrator (i.e. another communication course or mediation) than question their faith in the infallible hierarchy. My suggestion that rotating as opposed to permanent appointments be made to organising roles has been met with the same incredulous glassy stare that Galileo may have experienced when he championed an alternative heliocentric way of looking at the universe nearly 400 years ago.

Perhaps you are wondering what your own anti-bullying policy looks like? I doubt it runs to over a hundred pages like the UK Military of Defence bullying and harassment complaints procedures for both civilian and service personnel (MOD JSP, 2013). As noted in Chapter 6, *rule-based* policies tend to be specific and lengthy, especially when they are working on the assumption that *what is not forbidden is permitted*. In the case of an organisation with a rigid hierarchical structure whose *raison d'être* is defence (a euphemism for aggression) then a rule-based approach makes perfect sense.

It is good practice, nevertheless, for an organisation to do as much as possible to clarify its anti-bullying policies and thereby limit the role of management subjectivity that all too often becomes subverted into malign control.

What lies behind the angry smile?

Several years delivering psychoeducational courses on anger management for various counselling services led me to understand that people are very uncomfortable with anger in all its forms. More recently, working with anger from a H&S perspective, I noticed how this most visceral of emotions is treated much like any other hazard, like tripping over a loose piece of carpet. Overt aggression at work can be addressed through formal, albeit palliative, disciplinary procedures. Yet, for those attending my workshops, interest lay more in the covert manifestations of rage, or what participants called *rage in disguise*. What often lurks behind the façade of pleasantness and forbearance, especially for nice people in healthcare, religious communities, social work, and education are the destructive forces of anger (Alexander, 1975; Graham, 2007). In acknowledging the destructive effects of relational aggression, professional bodies, such as the BACP, tackle the issue head on through their Guidelines for Good Practice: "professional relationships will be conducted in a spirit of mutual respect ... endeavouring to build good working relationships and systems of communication ...".

Because the "nice" perpetrator must not betray the common behaviours associated with aggression, the healthy expression of anger becomes stifled like a yawn. Beneath the veneer of apparent compliance and appropriate behaviour, anger and resentment are expressed through a range of practices in the workplace including sabotage (e.g. poor punctuality, deliberate mistakes, and procrastination, or the accidental disclosure of sensitive information), seemingly innocent misunderstandings (*sorry … but I thought you knew!*), and apathy (*I'm fine … whatever!*) (McIlduff & Coghlan, 2000). The targets of passive aggression can feel confused and even guilty when tangling with a perpetrator, concluding that the anger that they experience in fact belongs to them. If you revisit the exchange between Helen and Tony in Chapter 4 (Box 4.4), you will notice how Tony engages in a passive form of aggression, which finally draws Helen in, who finally snaps and loses her temper in a more obvious and overt way. By postponing or avoiding confrontation with the perpetrator, the confusing experience of being a target of passive aggression can continue indefinitely, as in the case of Wendy in Box 7.5.

Box 7.5 Passive aggression

"I really don't like working with Wendy … she seems like a team player … saying all the right things … but then she keeps making quite serious 'mistakes' … as if she was inept … which undermines us all. And then she asks me if I'm cross with her … I mean … I am … but I avoid giving her a piece of my mind because … well … I feel guilty about being angry … she's so nice and caring in other ways … but there is something child-like about her that seems too fragile for her to take it in."

What motivates a perpetrator such as Wendy? Is it possible that she is retaliating against feeling like a target herself? A trigger for passive aggression could be the fear of "rocking the boat", which Dana Jack believes might be linked to gendered attitudes to relationships which see conflict as something that threatens to undermine or cause irreparable ruptures to our relationships (1999). The presumption that open conflict is somehow unhelpful only fuels avoidance and covert anger, which carries fewer risks of retaliation (see, Chapter 3, Tolerating the cycle of rupture and repair). The threat of change also evokes anxiety and fear for some, which is managed through either thwarting or undermining what is new. Perhaps Wendy learnt to be afraid of outward displays of strong emotions in childhood: "*nice girls just don't do that sort of thing*" – which is a powerful introject.

Irrespective of Wendy's motives, angry, hostile, or punitive responses by either her peers or managers will only make things worse. It is useful to recognise that bystanders become seduced into acting out the anger that apparently nice folk like Wendy decline to do for themselves (i.e. and Tony, see Box 4.4). This invites further retaliation and an inevitable downward spiral. All of us exhibit passive aggression from time to time, and depending on the context it can be healthy or perhaps even revolutionary. Peaceful protest and disobedience in the face of oppressive forces are examples of a healthier form of *rage in disguise*. Nonviolent civil rights movements led by figures such as Martin Luther King Jr and "Mahatma" Gandhi represent constructive, passive, and indirect aggression against overwhelming opposition. Increasing our self-awareness of the role of fear and anxiety in motivating people to act – or not act in the case of passivity – liberates us from the perpetual cycle of unhealthy relational abuse (Box 7.6).

Box 7.6 Responding to the rage behind the smile

Is there someone in your working life with whom you would like to bring things to the surface? Consider what you might say to them using the following structure using a supportive colleague*, mentor,* or supervisor* to rehearse.

1.   Reveal how this person affects you.
2.   Share hunches about their behaviour towards you.
3.   Invite them to talk about it.
4.   Say this to your partner* as if they are that person.
5.   Your partner* reacts and helps you modify if necessary.

   Would you risk using this approach in a real situation? What might stop you?
   *See Chapter 5.

The ethics of bystanding

Before we get too worthy about this, let us remember that the corruption complex is what everybody else does – right? It describes practices and behaviours that we fall foul of, or from which we are excluded or fail to profit. We are often content to ride the wave of corruption until it is our turn to take a tumble. Only then do we denounce such practices as corrupt. Those of us who legitimize our corrupt behaviours do so by blaming a system that gives us little choice because it rewards us for behaving in this way – an "*it is the only game in town*"- type of argument. The impunity with which figureheads in organisations enable corrupt behaviour usually invites the condemnation of their challengers, reciting sentiments such as: "I'm one of the good guys/gals … there are much worse out there then me, and you wouldn't want them in charge". In this way, unethical behaviour is justified because it helps fulfil important goals for the organization. As we have already seen, the time-served employee will even offset their corrupt acts by asserting they have "earned" the right to behave in ways that exploit others.

The corruption complex rarely results from the actions of just one employee and instead stems from the cooperation of several or even groups of people. Bystanders go along with unethical activities in the hope that they will benefit from the phenomenon of homosocialisation. Other organisational pressures such as league tables/performance indicators unintentionally fan the flames of corruption and a gaming of the system. Because we are all "up to it", the risk of being punished fails to deter. The research literature – and the media – are full of examples of the corruption complex in action, across public health, business, banking, the police, at all levels of education, politics, and the judiciary (Vickers, 2014). It is not easy to speak truth to power when you think something wrong is happening, especially as a vulnerable employee, i.e. in a non-unionised workplace. Sometimes things happen too quickly, especially in purposefully disorientating time-sensitive processes. For example, on leaving a job interview for an internal position in her company, Qian was taken-aback to see Mo waiting to go in next (Box 7.7).

Box 7.7 Banality of corruption

"I couldn't put my finger on why I felt so surprised to see him there until about ten minutes after when I realised … he did not meet the essential criteria for the post. Of course … that's why I was surprised to see him … technically speaking he wasn't supposed to be there … and then I felt sickened and angry because I knew I didn't stand a chance … and I was right … he got the job. But it just feels too risky to say something … and what will it change anyway … I'll just come across as being a stroppy cow and then I'll never get promoted?"

It requires moral courage to "blow the whistle" on corruption where we see it. We accept the status quo, telling ourselves: "this is the real world", and fail to act for a variety of reasons (Linstead, 2007):

- *It is easier to stick our heads in the sand.* This option offers limitless scope for ignoring the banality of injustice and psychological abuse around us. We can create our own stories to defend, mask or divert attention away from doing something about what we acknowledge to be wrong: "Nah … I don't see myself as a union man/woman", "I'm too busy", "what's the point", or "I'm alright Jack". Our excuse for not acting or speaking boldly for the common good might be because it involves too much risk to ourselves, our popularity, or our chances of promotion. This only allows the corruption complex to roll-on, unchecked, and ignores the fact that it is our response to corruption, and not the risk of retribution, that will make a difference. We ignore the ethical dimensions of the *corruption complex* altogether and see

Figure 7.4 Facing up to your stories.

each unfolding incident in terms of an isolated and unfortunate event that does not affect me … until finally it does, at which point we seek help and support, assuming we are lucky enough to have it to call on.

• *We sell ourselves a different story.* Not everything we see is so obvious, and the temptation to reframe our view of the world is compelling (e.g. *self-gaslighting*). We must trust ourselves about what we see even if we initially doubt our interpretation of events. Bystanding is deeper than simply seeing and failing to act. The ethical difficulty of being a bystander extends to our failure to examine, reflect on, and investigate what we feel, see, or experience. It is interesting that trade union membership tails off the higher up the hierarchy we climb. Too many compromises are required as one submits to the corruption complex.

Nothing changes when we defend ourselves against thinking and feeling when in the corruption complex. It is lazy and disappointing to do nothing and stand by, telling ourselves "but I live in the real world". Standing by as we witness behaviour that we know to be wrong whittles away at our own self-respect: we break the *Golden Rule* of ethical reciprocity (Box 5.5). The real world need not be characterised by shabby morals and rubbish behaviour. It is just as much about integrity, affection, respect, and reciprocity, not just the exploitation of others and making money. To paraphrase Michel de Montaigne, whose outlook feels as relevant today as it did 400 years ago, the importance of living and working to a higher moral code is to be able to "*face our stories as we get older*". Our attitudes to integrity, and the importance of reflectivity in guiding our journey through and beyond the world of paid work, are examined in the final chapter.

Things to keep in mind

- The corruption complex, whilst by no means a barrel of laughs, does at least give us an alternative to pathologising individuals.
- Euphemisms for relational abuse distract, disguise, or even excuse what is really going on.
- Organisational policies distract our gaze towards a reductionist, individualistic understanding of relational abuse.
- Gaslighting seduces us into questioning whether we can even trust ourselves to see what is going on.
- The *real world* of relationships involves integrity, affection, respect, and reciprocity. We do not have to accept the world of work as some cocktail of grubby corruption, exploitation, and cynicism.
- We have choices. Do not become isolated in the workplace. Triangulate perspectives, seek the advice of trusted colleagues, professional groups outside the organisation, or better still become active in your trade union.

References

Abramson K. (2014). Turning up the lights on gaslighting. *Philosophical Perspectives*, 28(1), 1–30.

Alexander CJ. (1975). Is "nice" nurse concealing passive aggression? *AORN Journal*, 21(7), 1179–1182.

Burrow S. (2005). The political structure of emotion: From dismissal to dialogue. *Hypatia*, 20(4), 27–43.

Foucault M. (1977). *Discipline and punish: The birth of the prison.* London: Allen Lane.

Graham A. (2007). The worm in the bud: Passive aggression in Christian communities. *The Furrow*, 58(11), 590–596.

Hutchinson M, Vickers, M, Jackson, D, & Wilkes L. (2006). Workplace bullying in nursing: Towards a more critical organizational perspective. *Nursing Inquiry*, 13(2), 118–126.

Jack DC. (1999). *Behind the mask: Destruction and creativity in women's aggression.* Cambridge, MA: Harvard University Press.

Liefooghe A & Mackenzie Davey K. (2010). The language and organization of bullying at work. *Administrative Theory & Praxis*, 32(1), 71–95.

Linstead S. (2007). The Comedy of Ethics: The New York four, the duty of care and organizational bystanding. In R Westwood & C Rhodes (Eds.), *Humour, Work and Organization* (chapter 11, pp. 203–231). London: Routledge.

Lutgen-Sandvik P, Tracy SJ, & Alberts JK. (2007). Burned by bullying in the American workplace: Prevalence, perception, degree and impact. *Journal of Management Studies*, 44(6), 837–862.

McIlduff E & Coghlan D. (2000). Understanding and contending with passive-aggressive behaviour in teams and organizations. *Journal of Managerial Psychology*, 15(7), 716–736.

MOD Bullying and Harassment Complaints Procedures. (2013). www.gov.uk/government/publications/jsp-763 [Accessed 1 November 2018].

Nielsen MB & Einarsen SV. (2018). An overview of the literature and agenda for future research. *Aggression and Violent Behaviour*, 42, 71–83.

Olivier de Sardan J-P. (1999). A moral economy of corruption in Africa? *The Journal of Modern African Studies*, 37(1), 25–52.

Pollert A & Charlwood A. (2009). The vulnerable worker in Britain and problems at work. *Work, Employment, and Society*, 23(2), 343–362.

Salin D, & Hoel H. (2013). Workplace bullying as a gendered phenomenon. *Journal of Managerial Psychology*, 28(3), 235–251.

Vickers MH (2014). Towards reducing the harm: Workplace bullying as workplace corruption – A critical review. *Employee Responsibility and Rights Journal*, 26, 95–113.

Chapter 8

Adjusting to life's crises

Change and identity

Good endings come before good beginnings. Biology is not destiny. The *epigenetic* revolution underway in the life sciences acknowledges that both our environment and genetics co-act in our development; we are the product of nature and nurture. Attachment theory similarly frames our life journey as a weaving together of our corporeal (i.e. genes, endocrine systems, and neural networks) and social selves in the avoidance of danger; a task ultimately doomed to failure. The Danish psychoanalyst Erik Erikson (1902–1994) adopted a slightly more upbeat view of our life course, seeing it instead as a series of profoundly rich developmental phases up to and including death. Change, he believed, was never easy: it disrupts, disorientates, causes us grief, and takes time to readjust. All transitions mean an ending of one sort or another, and endings are intrinsic to Erikson's model, which is why I believe it to be a useful framework for thinking about the arc of our working lives. Although not an enthusiast of stage models, I recognise as a counsellor and a human being the self-evident truth that a good ending must come before an equally good beginning. Erikson's appreciation of the cyclical pattern of life's endings and beginnings is therefore a powerful way to make sense of the disorientation we experience with life's transitions such as redundancy, career change, becoming a parent or carer, illness, disability, retirement, bereavement, and so on. This is especially relevant for those of us who work in organisations so often predicated on the avoidance and denial of the inevitability of endings (i.e. *Organisational Rituals* in Chapter 6).

Erikson's view of his fellow human beings was positive, mirroring Rogers' own humanistic perspective of life as something possessing a directional *actualising tendency* that drives us to expand, extend, develop and mature. Perhaps it was because he lived such a peripatetic and multicultural existence that Erikson saw life as a series of *identity crises*, resolved only through adapting to the necessities of our social, ethnic, historical, and political environments. He recognised how our development is embedded in a relational context that evolves over time. Although *crisis* literally means a turning point or period of difficulty, it more often than not sets off alarm bells when that word is used. I prefer to think instead of a crisis being a crossroads, which presents a dilemma that may or may not be resolved, but is nevertheless intrinsic to our journey. Our sense of incongruence, or feeling we are not our best selves, comes about when we become stuck at a crossroads, a sensation compounded when the institutions, people, or the cultural practices that ordinarily support us through these times are no longer there for us.

Although Erikson's model is often interpreted as being a set of ladder-like stages to be resolved before moving onto the next rung, he in fact grasped the circularity of life and how we continually return to resolve familiar difficulties. This seems obvious to me when we consider the turn of the seasons, the ebb and flow of tides, economic conditions, or the déjà vu sensation of the latest initiative in the workplace. If we are awake to it, we will see how issues have a way of coming around, repeatedly, in an uninterrupted flow from one part of our lifespan to another. A sense of unfinished business is common to the experience of endings, such as redundancy for example, where the unspoken anger, the unheard distress, and the embarrassed goodbyes seem to open old wounds from the past. We invariably think of only negative events that trigger disorientation and sometimes-painful readjustments at work. The anti-climax of achieving a long sought-after career goal can be equally disorientating, bringing to mind the dog who noisily chases a moving car, only to be nonplussed and confused when it finally "catches" the vehicle as it comes to a stop. If we can understand why we find being still so painful, we might learn to resolve the crisis of needing to chase our own metaphorical moving cars.

The *gestalt* perspective is a powerful and complementary approach for understanding the cycles of human experience which, when interrupted, evoke that nagging sensation of dissatisfaction, or as we like to call it *unfinished business*. The cycle of experience begins (if we allow it), with a growing *awareness* of some hunger or unmet need, like an itch in need of a scratch, perhaps seeking the thrill of the chase, or pursuing the next step on the career ladder, i.e. running after the metaphorical car. This is followed by implementing *actions* that help us seize our quarry by, say, working hard for that promotion. The moment of *climax* arrives as we achieve our goal, win our prize, or have things work out the way we want them. The next phase of *satisfaction* is where we allow ourselves time to savour our accomplishment before *withdrawing* and letting go of the task in order to make space for some new hunger to come into our awareness, often called the *fertile void*. This final phase can be the most uncomfortable one to be still with, because the temptation to act and literally "get on with" our next distracting activity is too powerful. Our inability to allow the cycle to reach completion nudges out the time we need for new *sensations*, ideas, or kernels of creativity to emerge into *awareness* once more. However, the fertile void is the place in which we can allow our good or satisfying endings to occur.

In *Identity and the Life Cycle*, Erikson introduces us to the idea of two broad phases of our development, namely *child* and *adult*, summarised in Box 8.1 (1980). The often tumultuous adolescent part of our development bridges these two phases. The tasks of adolescence are not slavishly located in this chronological period, but instead describe a lifelong preoccupation often triggered by social and personal experiences intersecting our lives, including work. It is the tricky and sometimes painful business of searching for a sense of who we are through exploring our values, beliefs, and goals. It involves the task of renegotiating a coherent sense of who we are, or who we want to be, through reflection on our past, present, and future. Before turning our attention to how Erikson's crisis of identity weaves with our working lives, I will to say more about the tasks of adolescence.

Box 8.1 Our crises of identity

The *childhood* phase mirrors the evolution of our attachment strategies, requiring a resolution of the tension between the following polarities (Kerpelman & Pittman, 2018).

Trust versus *Mistrust*. This forms the foundation of our emotional capacity for hope. It is a time when we develop a sense of our *own* trustworthiness, as well as our capacity to trust in others and recognise the world is an OK place.

Autonomy versus *Shame*. Our sense of autonomy developed in childhood reflects our obligations of compliance and the privileges of self-determination in adulthood. As we learn to explore and toddle, we encounter minor failures, meeting shame and self-doubt for the first time.

Initiative versus *Guilt*. As we learn to walk and be creative, we establish the conviction: *I am what I can imagine myself to be*, a notion indispensable to our development as adults. However, it becomes equally obvious that our infant-like ideals do not match up to adult realities. We experience guilt as we discover our actions may have a negative effect on others.

Industry versus *Inferiority*. Our early school years are when we take on board introjects and assumptions about the division of labour and how our worth is evaluated. Although this is a time to develop our sense of competence and industry, an over-emphasis on work leads to linking worth with compliance, conformity, and productivity.

At the heart of *adulthood* is the need to obtain and sustain our developed sense of identity. We do this through fostering intimacy, closeness, concern for others, and responsibility for the choices we have made, again by resolving the tension between the following polarities.

Intimacy versus *Isolation*. Only when we have developed a coherent sense of who we are can we engage in true intimacy beyond our immediate families. Merger with another requires confidence that we will not be overwhelmed. A fragile sense of self will see intimacy as something risky, and our fear of identity annihilation leads to isolation and self-absorption.

Generativity versus *Stagnation*. The primary concern here is to be the originator of others – either literally or metaphorically – and the generator of things and ideas that contribute to society. This is the counterpoint to stagnation, where boredom, interpersonal impoverishment, and a loss of purpose or meaning in our lives feels it may not be far away.

Integrity versus *Despair*. The final stage can be one of emotional integration, when we reflect on our life journey, becoming satisfied and at peace with our old age, or alternatively despairing about our physical decline and the reality of death.

Adolescence is a lifelong project of synthesis, integration and evolution. Our need to be reflexive and our capacity to adapt to change has never been more important than now, given our longer lives and increasingly complex social settings. How can we accept ourselves if we are unsure of who we are, how we seem to others, and whether we can commit to our relationships, ideas, or values? Understanding who we are requires ongoing work to understand ourselves in relation to our social contexts, recognising, as Karl Marx implored, that we need not sleepwalk through our lives. The pervasiveness of our consumer-driven culture and the growing individualisation of our life choices challenge us to regularly reinvent ourselves. Yet the cult of the synthesised person is a special danger to us all, because we are more than what we buy or how we wish to appear on social media. Many of us have working lives very different from those of our parents, so we can no longer rely on them as models for how to respond to our evolving selves. Although stereotypes seem like useful guides, they are not. What a *man* or *woman* used to do is no longer helpful to us when looking to the future.

Yet many of us live relatively satisfying lives without feeling the need to engage in the difficult and sometimes painful task of reflexivity. After all, "we are not paid to be ourselves at work", I hear you say, "I am paid to put on a face and hide my authentic self". But what is the cost of incongruence? Perhaps you or someone you know becomes anxious or even impatient with others in times of uncertainty, becoming frustrated and angry when they do not "get on with it". Do you have a strong, unquestioning commitment to who you are, swallowed whole from institutions (i.e. organised religion, school, or university) or figures of authority (dominant parents, teachers, etc.) early in life? Are you or someone you know living life in a dissociated haze of consumption, social media, televised sport, or driven to "organise" the world around them to keep busy, seduced into what Buddhists refer to as the cyclic existence? When you find yourself stressed, is it because some aspect of your inflexible life plan refuses to yield to your control? Do you feel like going off the rails when your neatly constructed version of the world is threatened? Does the organisation or a colleague get the blame when your environment does not adapt to you? When challenged about the way you see the world, do you react with defensiveness or rage, exposing your brittle self-esteem ordinarily camouflaged by bluster?

Being stuck in this way, unable to process and manage change, might indicate you are stuck in a part of your cycle. Reflexivity is a challenging process for us all, because it forces us to question what we know and how we have come to know it. It need not be something we do on our own, and is in fact a process that can be promoted through the safe and holding environments offered by mentors, supervisors, and other supportive communities, so long as we reach out and access them.

Identity, reflexivity, and the world of work. I want to examine next how the polarities or Erikson's crises intersect with events across our working lives (Osborne, 2009). You should take a closer look at Box 8.1 before reading on, because I am not attempting to provide an exhaustive account of our existential crises – you may wish to add a few of your own? For me, though, it seems that two of the big three emotions that protect us from danger, namely fear and shame, inform and even drive the denial, avoidance, or even the healthy processing of our existential crises.

A lack of *trust* in ourselves and our capacity to survive transitions in times of uncertainty can feel harrowing. In the case of retirement, for example, I have seen both white-knuckled terror and decision-making paralysis grip those who cannot trust themselves to *get it right* as they approach their occupational death. Younger workers can also experience a similar freeze/flop response as they realise that the apparent certainties of their goals and ambitions are in fact introjects, swallowed whole from their parents, peers, or teachers. We feel disillusioned and lost as we stumble off the travellator of somebody else's dreams, wondering, *what next?* High levels of anxiety and fear for both groups can lead to either impulsive decision-making or drastic changes in direction. If unresolved, the pattern of rashness and indecision can stretch beyond the young-worker stage, which I discuss later, into retirement, where more crossroads and shorter timescales raise the stakes.

A diminished sense of *autonomy*, brought about through the loss of something important to us such as a role or job, changes to our health, or retiring before a partner, can bring with it feelings of *shame* as we feel our intrinsic value ebb away. Going to work and feeling involved in the business of *production* is habitual, and if we are not involved and feel left behind somehow, we struggle to find what gives us new value and meaning in our lives.

The question of: "what to do with the rest of my life", feels less intimidating in the flush of youth, when we are better able to face the problem of grasping the *initiative* with enthusiasm and energy. Even if we do feel "left behind", having swallowed whole the timetables and career expectations set by our institutions and peers, there is still time to resolve our sense of guilt, shame, or inadequacy about not keeping up. At the gloaming of our lives, on losing a job, with the kids leaving home, or retiring for whatever reason, we may feel unable to summon the energy to embark on a new phase with the same vim and vigour as before. Some of us do not encounter this wavering of initiative, finding ourselves busier than ever through unpaid and arguably more valuable work in our communities. We refuse to throw in the towel and give up, much like Santiago in Hemmingway's *The old man and the sea*, proclaiming defiantly *I can be destroyed … but not defeated.*

Industriousness is more than the relatively modest task of searching for our daily bread, but is about pursuing a "life other than a Monday to Friday sort of dying" (Terkel, 1974). Once we accept the idea of work as something meaningful and not just about earning money, then we need not worry about industriousness, especially in retirement. We can do more with our time than putting our feet up or immersing ourselves in hobbies, recreation, or travel. We soon realise that being involved in something meaningful is more important than mindlessly keeping busy filling our days with empty tasks, Sudoku, and tidying. These activities defend against the nagging anxiety that we are not just looking for a job, but a calling.

Erikson's original intention when reflecting on *intimacy* was to address the readiness of young adults for love, marriage, and family life. For younger workers, an authentic sense of belonging to a team, group, or organisation requires first an understanding of who we are. A woman who has spent her early years doing the work of reproduction and childrearing is understandably reluctant to retire simply because her male partner has had enough and needs entertaining at home. When retirement arrives in a partnership where there exists a significant age gap between the two, difficulties can arise when unexpected levels of independence, solitude, or perhaps social isolation are suddenly enforced on the one who "stays at home". Relationships are tested, sometimes to destruction, when we achieve our goal of retiring early. The work-based networks of validation and habitual structure, so important in shaping our identity when at work, are suddenly swept away, leaving us feeling disoriented and vulnerable. It was only after retirement and the loss of his partner that Carl Rogers was truly able to integrate, through contact groups and other intimate relationships, a more authentic sense of who he was (Kirschenbaum, 2007). *Must we leave it so late to be who we truly are?* Can you accept you have many deficiencies and faults, can make mistakes, are ignorant where you should be knowledgeable, are prejudiced when you should be open-minded, and have feelings that are not always justified by the circumstances?

Our capacity for industry is essential for success during any exhilarating transition. We can find ourselves flat out in the meaningful *generative* work of being grandparents, carers, training to become counsellors, or volunteering as a teacher or mentor at work. Retirees do, however, experience ageism even from their own families, who dismiss new projects such as retraining as a "hobby" rather than the next stage of a person's generative life development. The risk for the generative person is burning out, because the better we get at caring for others, the more others (and we) expect from ourselves.

Stagnation is something that can emerge at any stage of our working lives; our hunger to be satisfied with what we do says more about who we are than the task itself. Our generativity can be blocked when we do not have a project or someone to care for, which means events such as being side-lined at work, be it paid or unpaid, retiring or becoming unemployed starves us of the nourishing rewards for our proven capacity to give to others. *Pseudo-generativity* is essentially *Rescuing*, discussed earlier in the context of the Drama Triangle (Chapter 4). What can seem at first to be altruism comes with strings attached.

All the other stages of our lives have a sense of building towards a future; the crisis of *integrity*, however, requires us to accept both the past and the inevitable end. How do we retain a vital sense of who we are when those we have cherished and invested in are departing with increasing frequency, through either moving onto a new role, outright retirement, or their death? Those of us who have worked a notice period at work will be aware of just how quickly we become invisible or irrelevant to those we will soon leave behind. It is a reminder of how the workplace is the context that we use to structure our meanings, and when it becomes unavailable, the affirming context for our identities disappears too. We shrink and become less visible. Confronted with dwindling visibility, we are thrown back onto our inner resources. We now have the time and permission to stop the endless *doing* of generativity and learn about the *being* of integrity. Some consider Richard Strauss to have been the greatest octogenarian composer of all time, because it was at the age of 84 that he created his sublime masterpiece *Four Last Songs*. A rough translation of a line from the original German text asks the question: *will summer smile amazed and exhausted on the dying dream that was your garden?*

A crisis in the face of despair need not wait until the latter parts of our working lives. As a young man, I worked in a factory making tin cans. The isolating impact of the production–line noise and the relentless monotony of the task in hand led me to breaking point, fleeing with tears of frustration after only a week. What triggered my reaction was a tea break with a particularly heroic man who explained how he had been doing the same job for over 30 years. What gave him meaning in his toil was that this was something he was doing for his growing family. That is when I learnt that unless I can derive meaning from my work, it becomes little more than *my* Monday to Friday kind of dying.

For the remainder of the chapter I want to reflect on the things we do not talk about at work. Getting older is never too much fun, and at a mundane level, I am struck by how few people like to celebrate their birthdays in the world of work. Yet, getting older is considerably better than the alternative. Chronologically older and younger workers mix in the workplace, and I want to consider what we think as we watch others: *Go gently into that good night?* Life is pain – as the Buddha taught us – and work is full of life – so where is the space to reflect on *Loss, Grief,* and *Trauma?* Some of us work in the caring professions, but many more of us care beyond our paid work. What are the tensions and difficulties of *Caring for Vulnerable Others?* Finally, having identified what needs to change, I ask whether there is an upside to seeing the old guard disappear from the workplace, and whether we can afford to wait for *change to happen one retirement at time.*

Occupational death: going gently into that good night

Puppy for the path, dog for the road. In addition to my name and other things, my paternal grandfather passed onto me a life-stage model that took the form of a deliciously dark ditty:

Twenty young
Thirty strong
Forty good as ever
Fifty old
Sixty cold
Seventy gone forever!

The sentiment behind the rhyme reflects the expectations of generations passed, inured to hard physical labour and without access to the healthcare we enjoy today. For this reason, I feel many are lucky enough to recalibrate the rhythm to begin at *Thirty Young?* But the flipside is that our healthier, longer lives have caused a demographic shift in our population that we can no longer afford. The Pension Policy Institute projects that one in three UK residents (and one in four in the USA) will be of state retirement age by 2030, which amounts to a total spend on benefits to pensioners of more than £150 billion at today's prices. As the school leaving age effectively creeps into our early twenties, it is clear the proportion of older workers must increase. The removal of the Default Retirement Age (DRA) in the UK during 2011 went some way towards achieving this; employees are no longer made redundant because of their age. Employers have to either decide on a justified retirement age, or operate without a retirement age altogether. This brings with it new challenges for organisations and employees alike. More than ever, it is essential that if possible, we remain in the workplace by maintaining and promoting our capacity for work.

For those of us currently over 50 who began their working lives when retirement at 60 was a reasonable expectation, this feels like a rip off. To paraphrase my favourite curmudgeon Philip Larkin, at 55 being *neither rich nor dead, find I have to work instead*. Now that the goal posts have shifted – from 60 to 66 for women – a 50-year-old has at least 16 years ahead of them until they can collect their state pension. Those 16 years, for a 22-year-old graduate, are in principle times of exciting career advancement. Yet for a 50-year-old, with all manner of prejudices, responsibilities, and perceptions to bear, the future may not seem quite so exciting.

Unjustified age discrimination appears rife in spite of it being illegal in the EU. Polling commissioned in 2017 by Age UK found that 36% of older workers (i.e. those over 50) felt they had been disadvantaged at work because of their age. The picture is, I believe, complex and possibly more hopeful than these statistics imply. You will remember in Chapter 4 how I described the way our blind spots come about through the gap between our self-perceptions and how others actually see us. The same idea can be extended to groups, which in this case refers to younger, middle-aged, or older workers i.e. ages 18–30, 31–50, and over 50, respectively. Blind spots lie in the gap between our *stereotypes* (i.e. what a younger worker presumes to be true about older colleagues) and *meta-stereotypes* (i.e. what a younger worker presumes an older colleague thinks about them). Stereotypes shape how we treat others, but meta-stereotypes affect how we *expect* to be treated, and how we behave in response to those expectations.

When asked what they believed younger people thought about them, older ones came up with some unattractive characteristics, including boring, old, stubborn, and grumpy (Finkelstein *et al.*, 2013). However, this is not what the younger ones *actually* think about their older colleagues. Despite the popular myth that older workers are maligned by callow youth, the opposite is true. Older workers may be surprised to learn that younger ones think about them more positively, as responsible, mature, and hard-working. The younger cohort, on the other hand, have bleak expectations of how they are seen by their elders. In the case of the middle-aged group, their suspicions are sadly accurate, whereas older workers are far more positive and optimistic about the traits of their younger colleagues. Perhaps this is because older workers are far more interested in career homeostasis, which is to say, we are less interested than middle-aged workers in personal competition and the relentless drive for promotion, valuing instead the work of generativity and legacy building (Box 8.2; Steinhauser *et al.*, 2009).

The conclusion of research, then, is that older and younger groups in the workplace have more to offer each other than they presume to be the case, and that the former need to be convinced that this is so. Older workers choosing to take on the role of supervisor or mentor are simply engaging in the stage-appropriate tasks of homeostasis: *being* as opposed to *doing*. Therefore, it is time to dispense with the bog standard, one-size-fits-all professional development review, useful for those new to the world of work, but less so for those who have been on the road for some time.

We must acknowledge how our life stage shapes both our view of the world and the tasks that interest us; a notion reflected in the proverb oft used by my father, which introduced the section.

Box 8.2 A pause for thought

The arc of my working life. An opportunity to reflect on my strengths and values, reviewing my experience of work as a *whole*.

- If another were to re-tell the story of my working life, what would be the most important things to include?
- What are my most cherished moments or times?
- Which of my achievements am I most proud of?

A matter of forgiveness. A chance to reflect and weigh up whether I am at peace with the experiences of my working life.

- If I were to do things again, what might I do differently?
- Are there things or times I regret?
- Is there anyone from whom I would like to either ask or offer forgiveness?

Heritage and legacy-building. A chance to wonder about what comes next.

- What are the most valuable lessons I have learned?
- What would I like to share with those who will come after me?
- If I could choose one thing as my legacy, what would it be?

Loss, grief, and trauma at work

"It's not personal ... it's strictly business." As the fictional mobster Michael Corleone of *The Godfather* ominously proposes, endings and transitions mean wholly different things to those involved, especially in the world of *business*, however we define it. I was told by my parents of the time they visited their village cemetery to choose a plot for their final resting place. My father noticed the gravedigger taking a break, so being pragmatic about such matters he approached and asked where, in his opinion, was the best place to be buried. The gravedigger quickly pointed to a corner they had not considered up to that point. "What's so special about there?" my father asked. "Well, that's where the digging's easiest", came the reply.

A simple example of how someone's world view, rendered narrow by the constraints of their work, can be experienced as indifference at best, or inhumane at worst. Similarly, organisations can and do become detached from their humanity in pursuit of a flexible workforce, a euphemism for creeping casualisation characterised by zero-hours contracts, frequent restructuring, forced retirements/resignations and redundancy. The spectre of inhumanity and the emotional vandalism committed by one another haunts the corridors of our workplaces. The planned obsolescence embedded in the fabric of what we do, the services we provide, and the things we buy and sell casts its own shadow of being excess to requirements in a world already full of things we do not need. So why should our organisations reframe their priorities to embrace its humanity and abandon the inexorable drive for flexibility which ultimately spells the end for us all? Even the otherwise grumpy Philip Larkin reminds us in *The Mower* about the harm we cause through our carelessness: *be careful of each other, we should be kind while there is still time.* Perhaps the answer is simple: showing compassion to each other at work avoids *survivor syndrome.* Those who survive and are witness to how colleagues are treated, with either indifference or unfairness, understandably feel less secure and loyal towards their organisations (Vinten & Lane, 2002). For those who live by the sword, the world of work becomes a lonely and friendless place, and much like the gravedigger in my story, retirement offers little comfort, being spent instead in an alcoholic fug ruminating on *who will bury him?*

The pain of everyday working life. Because we spend so much time at work, it is inevitable that at any given time we will be alongside someone who is experiencing the pain of loss. A wall of silence often insulates those who grieve in the workplace. Often, well-meaning actions of the concerned lead to a colleague's pain being unacknowledged or perhaps denied. A manager who felt they were being thoughtful circulated an email to the team insisting that nobody was to mention Beryl's miscarriage when she returned to work because it might upset her. At the other extreme, Ashok goes missing for a month and management feel they are protecting him by explaining that something so terrible has happened that they could not possibly say. Beryl and Ashok are entitled to their privacy, but is it also true that they may have welcomed compassion and support on their return, as opposed to embarrassed silence and gossip? When confronted by someone else's pain we can become frozen into inaction, frightened of getting it wrong when attempting to support a colleague return to work after their loss. It might explain why there is so little research or attention paid to human pain at work, although the workplace merely amplifies our broader sense of discomfort with the pain of others in our society (Thompson & Thompson, 2009).

We have assumed it is a matter of offering a grieving colleague a period of compassionate leave to just get over things, so that they can return to work restored to their former selves. Yet grief is a road that does not lead to our old selves. It is a process that takes time through which we must learn to hold those we lose in loving memory. Our identity and inner status change as we learn to integrate the legacy of those we lose in our ongoing lives (Klass *et al.*, 1996). There can be no fixed formula for understanding the time taken to resolve the pain of rejection and loss; emotional numbing and grief are felt for days, months, or years. Failing to secure promotion, losing a job, a partner (through divorce or the breakdown of a relationship), or the unimaginable pain of losing a child all take their toll in ways we find hard to predict. A colleague can return to work outwardly unaffected by the death of a partner or parent because their relationship with the deceased was indifferent or distant. Yet, the loss of a much-loved pet can trigger profound and life-shattering grief.

Rituals that support the transformation between the paradoxical stations of moving on and letting go are all but absent in the workplace. The contradiction between the two is inexplicable yet necessary, sitting uneasily in the neat, orderly, and controlled scientific paradigm of the modern workplace. Whatever the loss, it will not be soothed through mechanistically applied HR policies. Healing requires a supportive work culture, not just an automatic referral to six sessions of counselling through the company employee assistance programme (EAP). Concrete and tangible assistance means support over time, giving someone the space to be heard if they want it, and ongoing care and concern because although we may forget about someone's loss in a month or two, they will not. Rituals and ceremonies help express feelings and legitimise what we have lost. A CEO who built a multinational company working on his own from a pokey office 30 years previously retired. Detailed succession planning and a handover period along with a series of celebrations and parties marked his ending. After acting as a consultant for a while, he was able to slowly let go as the beginning of his *afterlife* had been ceremonially marked.

When a loss is too great, going on can feel like an overwhelming burden. Although suicide in the workplace is relatively uncommon, when it does occur not only is it a tragic loss of life, but it also has a lasting impact on colleagues. Those left behind can experience a complex mixture of emotions, which is why Business in the Community and Public Health England, for example, created resources for employers to help reduce the risk of suicide in the work-place (2017).

The trauma of everyday life. We think of occupational groups such as first responders, police officers, firefighters, healthcare professionals, etc. as being most at risk of experiencing stressful events that make them vulnerable to psychological trauma. Self- and employee-selection processes go some way to explain why those in high-risk occupations appear more resilient to traumatic stress than others. Yet the effects of trauma can be profound and disorientating because we experience the present with the physical sensations and emotions from the past. Traumatised people can be hypervigilant, experience flashbacks/nightmares, anxiety/panic attacks, and levels of absent-mindedness that causes difficulties with being fully engaged, seeming somewhat detached from the "present moment". The physical immobilisation of inescapable shock, where someone's fight/flight response is downregulated, manifests itself somatically through often-overlooked symptoms such as stomach upsets, aches, pains, irregular heartbeats, and so on.

The reality is that over half the adult population is exposed to a severe stressor at some point during our lives, and nearly everyone develops a post-traumatic stress reaction shortly after. Our bodies remember emergency surgical interventions, losing a pregnancy, life-threatening incidents, accidents, becoming a target of sexual or other physical assaults, and the vicarious trauma of being close to those who have lived through such events. A frightening or shocking event can have a shattering effect on our sense of living in an orderly and predictable world. Sudden or unexpected experiences such as emotional abuse, professional rejection, job loss or other dramatic changes in our circumstances can equally leave us unprepared to rebuild our trust in the world. Yet not all traumatic experiences need be stereotypically harrowing. It is generally assumed that becoming a parent is an irredeemably positive and lovely experience, and on the whole I would agree. Yet having worked therapeutically with families affected by perinatal depression in the past, I am reminded of how our current, narrow conceptualisation of trauma means we often underestimate the challenges of realigning who we are and how we think of ourselves after a significant life-altering event like becoming a parent. We overlook how we too must be born as parents when our children arrive.

The dilemma of working with trauma is that while a *Relational Approach* contains the cardinal elements of affect regulation, interpersonal trauma often results in a fear of intimacy (Box 8.3). The promise of relational contact automatically evokes memories of past hurt, betrayal, gaslighting, and abandonment. As a result, feeling understood, which ordinarily helps us to a greater sense of calm, can trigger trauma for those who have been hurt in intimate relationships. Understanding and working with trauma is as much about remembering and prizing how we survived than what has been broken within (Van der Kolk, 2006).

Box 8.3 I am not being difficult...I am traumatised

Martin took time off work for what he expected to be routine surgery for a back problem that had been niggling him. Unfortunately, the operation uncovered a serious underlying issue, which after further medical interventions left him with limited mobility. What began as a period of sick leave developed into a protracted and stressful negotiation with work about what could be done to help him perform his original role. Discussions with management became increasingly difficult as trust and patience on both sides became strained. Matters were not helped by the fact that Martin felt exhausted and angry with each encounter, and after a time he simply avoided contact with work. What nobody seemed to realise, or perhaps admit, was that he had been traumatised by his experience and was struggling to grieve his past, and realign with his new identity. Feeling disoriented by anger, fear, and shame is a normal reaction to grieving the loss of our identity. Coming to a place where we can usefully engage in the support offered is a process that requires time, patience, and support. What Martin needed to hear was: *this is a normal reaction to an abnormal experience, and you will do well given time and support* (Skogstad et al., 2013).

The bad news is ... there's no good news. Breaking bad news to someone is an emotionally difficult task that requires skill and training. Despite a snappy acronym to guide us through the process (i.e. SPIKE: Box 8.4), it is rarely a correspondingly linear experience (Baile *et al.*, 2000). In delivering bad news, we expect to trigger strong emotions in others such as anger, fear, shame, and grief. In their turn, the bearer of bad news may experience a mixture of their own and projected feelings of anxiety, guilt, doubt, and disappointment. When done insensitively, it becomes a potentially traumatising experience in itself and only adds to the woes of the recipient. The emotional cocktail can be unpalatable to the bearer of bad news too. Having accompanied colleagues to difficult meetings in the past, I have witnessed all too human managers attempt to simply survive the experience by disengaging, avoiding eye contact, typing, and staring implacably at their laptop throughout the interview, claiming when challenged that: "I can do two things at once".

Our reaction to bad news can be to adopt the fight, flight, or freeze behaviours, which are manifestations of our big three survival emotions of anger, fear, and shame. You may be disappointed to learn there is no quick fix to the distress brought about by the trauma of bad news. Only the patience and compassion of a *Relational Approach* will support those affected restore communication and group identity, regain a sense of empowerment through participation in work, and strengthen the expectation of feeling better in the future.

Box 8.4 Breaking bad news – the SPIKE approach

Setting up the interview. Attention to boundaries, such as privacy and other distractions including seating, should not be overlooked. It is important to ensure that a colleague or union representative supports the interviewee, but ultimately it is their choice. Adopting a *Relational Approach* is key to making a human connection with the interviewee. If you are not prepared to do this, then ask yourself why you have been given this role.

Perception. It is important to adopt the position: *before I tell, you can ask.* Explore whether the interviewee understands the context of the meeting and has an accurate appraisal of the facts. It is more empowering and addresses the implication that something is being "done to" them.

Invitation. Although denial is a valid coping mechanism, it is important to check with the interviewee whether they are ready to hear *all* the information you have to share at the time.

Knowledge-giving. Do this using straightforward language which avoids being insensitive or excessively blunt.

Empathy. This refers to a *Relational Approach*. Identifying, acknowledging, and empathising with a person addresses their need to be understood *in the moment*. This is the most difficult aspect of the process, because to be truly helpful, the interviewer must resist the temptation to engage in defensive rituals (Chapter 6).

Caring for vulnerable others

Parents caring for their children. The International Labour Organisation sees reconciling the gender gap between *paid* employment and *unpaid* caring and housework as perhaps the most significant social challenge of the twenty-first century. Yet, it seems remarkable to me that transformational experiences such as childbirth and becoming a parent are almost invisible at work despite the rise of women in the labour market. The parallel businesses of production and reproduction (i.e. family responsibilities and child development) seem neatly spliced by at least six months' maternity leave for women who remain the main providers of care for our children. Even beyond maternity leave, women are more likely to step back from paid work to do the heavy lifting of caring, resulting in what some call the "maternity penalty". Men can dip into the world of reproduction for as little as two weeks if they choose with one man explaining to me that he took the opportunity of paternity leave to go on holiday with his mates. Despite anecdotal evidence to the contrary, research suggests that there is a healthy level of take up of full statutory paternity leave in European countries (notably 80% in Norway, Finland, Sweden, and Spain with a length of 5, 3, 2 months, and 13 days, respectively), although fewer than 5% go beyond the statutory minimum. Research shows that *paternity leave*, where men engage in the work of *reproduction* for at least two weeks after childbirth, makes it more likely that they will be involved with their young children's lives. This in turn has a positive impact on their kids doing better in life on almost every indicator of success. The recognition of men's responsibility for sharing the work of reproduction will help change stereotypical attitudes and lead to greater equality for *both* men and women at work and at home. Greater engagement by men in the work of reproduction also minimises the maternity penalty on a women's career and her earning potential, and constitutes both a sustainable and structural resolution of the gender pay gap.

However, prejudice and soft penalties towards stereotypically feminine behaviour in men persist, especially for those belonging to the management caste, who try to go beyond the standard paternity leave (Gartzia *et al.*, 2018). And, as if matters were not already complicated enough, couples who flip traditional male earner/female primary carer roles out of either choice or necessity find that stay-at-home fathers are especially vulnerable to feelings of social isolation, shame, and stigma when attempting to engage in communities of carers where their sex is in the minority (Dunn *et al.*, 2013).

Children caring for their parents. Caring for our mothers, fathers, or indeed partners is a generative process – it is not just about caring for others, but about supporting them taking care of themselves in our communities. Much of the work of informal caregiving is invisible, time-consuming, exhausting, and from time to time distressing. It encompasses ongoing activities such as offering protection for those who may have lost their agency and autonomy and managing their households. Workers caring for their elderly parents, for example, do not receive the same levels of spontaneous excitement and legitimacy as those with obligations to their "bonnie bairns", with workers very often concealing their commitments from their employer. The majority of caregivers tend to be female, either daughters, daughters-in-law, or wives, who also experience parallel and significant life events such as getting married, having children and grandchildren, in addition to being professionally active. It is obvious, then, that carers who are fortunate enough to be in a workplace that emphasises flexible working, unpaid leave, using accumulated holidays or paid sick leave (see next) to help look after their parents are more likely to stay in the workforce.

It must be understood however, that the spheres of reproduction and production will remain "utterly incompatible" until the structural employment practices impeding doing gender differently are addressed (Miller, 2011). Until that time, all else is well-meaning window dressing.

***Swinging the lead?* Thinking differently about sick leave**. For many, attitudes to sick leave are somewhat black and white. There are those of us who understand that time off work is deserved because we have a legitimate need to recover from illness, injury, infection, or surgery, for example. The practice of "taking a sickie", on the other hand, seen by the disaffected worker as an effective way to increase leave entitlement, is a cynical means to avoid work; it exploits both the trust of the employer, and our colleagues who have to do the extra work in our absence. Between these two extremes lies a complex grey area where responsibility lies with neither a *bad* employee nor a *bad* manager.

Take, for example, the case of a worker who absents himself or herself from a workplace where they are the target of emotional abuse or some other psychological pressure. Attachment theory would see this as a perfectly reasonable strategy of *avoidance* to insulate the worker from a toxic environment. However, the approach offers only temporary relief, and is unlikely to lead to a long-term resolution because when the period of statutory sick leave ends, the problems lie in wait. When the worker enjoys protected status through union membership, for example, then the lazy resolution for the organisation is the increasingly popular NDA/exit deal that falls miserably short of the benefits of a sustainable, longer-term systemic outcome. The circumstance leading to the worker's sick leave remain unaddressed and so the toxic caravan trundles on.

When we are feeling fed up, overworked, stressed, or unappreciated, then a minor cold, a case of the sniffles, or some other minor ailment becomes what my Italian family refer to as: *é la goccia che fa traboccarea il vaso*, or "the drop that spills the vase". Taking a duvet day to recover from what we convince ourselves to be an entirely physical (somatic) ailment is our body's way of telling us enough is enough. Contemporary medicine is only beginning to understand the link between our emotional, somatic, cultural, and social selves. Pain, for example, does not distinguish between the somatic and psychological; it takes control of our whole being, and permeates our physical and emotional selves. The somatic manifestations of emotional distress remain enigmatic, often unexplained, and are rarely accounted for in a doctor's sick note. Presenteeism (Chapter 1) is often accompanied by a range of symptoms, such as joint pain, headaches, fatigue, trouble sleeping, poor appetite, weight change, palpitations, dizziness, nausea, loose bowels, gas/bloating, constipation, and abdominal pains (Eriksen & Risør, 2014). Sick leave becomes a way of life as the afflicted, perhaps out of awareness, literally embodies the emotional turmoil of their team or organisation.

A key question organisational representatives must ask if they are genuinely committed to promoting the wellbeing of their workers is: can we be confident that our culture is not a factor contributing to sickness absence? A simplistic and reductionist approach to managing sickness – the default setting for a busy manager – only invites technical fixes, such as increased bureaucratisation and MI assisted return-to-work programmes and the like. Unwell people are often being helped back into the same meat grinder that churned them out in the first place.

If we ignore what disturbs us, rush to pathologise the individual and ignore the context, then we take another step closer to ruin. So long as we insist on thinking about people as isolated components in a machine we will never break the cycle of denying the shadow cast by systemic causes. We are organic, relational, and wholly integrated in our systems. A holistic and sophisticated approach is required to move us away from seeing the "sick person" as the problem and the organisation as the innocent bystander or benign *Rescuer* (Chapter 7).

Change happens one retirement at a time

Much like our contemporary management caste, the nineteenth-century aristocrats described in Giuseppe di Lampedusa's novel *The Leopard* understood that to avoid a revolution they had to take the initiative because, "if we want things to stay as they are, things will have to change". Is this the kind of thinking that creates the façade of change to which we are regularly exposed? More staff surveys, the launch of another wellbeing strategy, the purchase of wellbeing products (i.e. access to EAPs, free eye tests, and flu jabs) including online courses suggesting how employees should make better lifestyle choices, i.e. "relax by looking at a flower or watch a child play". All this is notwithstanding the annual ruminations on return to work metrics by HR professionals and the like. Pathologising the employee as a failing cog in the machine only distracts us from the systemic features of the organisations that sicken us. The Nobel Prize-winning physicist Max Planck, who played a large part in formulating quantum theory, was asked how he revolutionised the way we see the world. His response went along the lines of the title to this section. Revolutions in thinking happen not because Lampedusa's aristocrats or Planck's sceptics were convinced by compelling arguments, but because they became extinct. We are living through a time of social disruption, global economic, environmental and public health crises and profound uncertainty, with dissatisfied workers looking for alternatives to the bonfire of social interests we created at the high altar of investment confidence. Can we afford to be distracted by the beer and circuses of mock change, or wait around for Max Planck's extinction model to take effect?

More training is the solution? The solution to almost every problem in an organisation seems to be: "*more training ... and preferably online*". Clearly, training is important, especially when it comes to technical competencies such as IT, H&S, data protection, and so on. It is equally important to realise, though, that training is something organisations "do" to their employees, either directly through the human resources department, or by some third-party sanctioned by management. The organisational hierarchy identifies a deficit in skills or behaviour (i.e. more effective leadership, greater alignment with stress management bureaucracy, dealing with difficult situations/people, emotional intelligence, influencing), *then* identifies a desired outcome for the training, i.e. performance is more effective, anger is managed, tough messages delivered, difficult situations/people dealt with. The liberalisation of the care market has seen a burgeoning of a freewheeling life-coach industry that anxiously seeks to meet the needs of their over-charged clients. Trainers approach the task from a reality shaped and created by those who commission their work. The ethos of the task, informed by neoliberal dogma, sees learning as a way to enable corporate capability, increasing cost-effectiveness and worker productivity. Training can thus fulfil the paradoxical purpose of per-petuating the myth that workers are malfunctioning or defective components of an otherwise efficient Taylorian machine. We can now understand encounters such as the one retold in Box 8.5, not simply in terms of the problematic nature of training, but through the lens of the previous chapters. Is this an example of a *Relational Approach*? While appearing to engage in a worthy project, what is Stan's actual agenda? Although he identifies "time" as the enemy, what, in terms of Bion's basic assumptions, does he really fear? What relationship style or ego state does he adopt during the session, and how might he do things differently? Will his current approach create real sustainable change, and what might be gained by trying a different approach? Or must we content ourselves with Stan's logic that it is better than doing nothing at all (i.e., gaslighting).

Box 8.5 *Firm management to the rescue*

Stan – a senior manager – is facilitating the company's anti-bullying group involving staff representatives and HR. To stop it becoming "a talking shop", he schedules one-hour quarterly meetings with clear objectives set out beforehand. Today, he's brainstorming the new role of "anti-bullying investigator", whose purpose is to be an impartial figure gathering evidence when accusations are being made. Using Post-Its Stan quickly covers a nearby wall with his thoughts, paying little heed to the discussion going on around him, finally adding: "We're making real pro-gress here don't you think? ... Some important themes emerging; let's see ... job description ... a serious role but not management ... obvi-ously, skills, selection, monitoring ...". A staff representative, Jane, tries to speak: "Can you really investigate gaslighting, passive aggression and all that as if it were a crime scene?" Stan cuts her off: "There's always evi-dence ... emails, stuff people say ... and besides ... investigators will be trained to be neutral ... they will know the difference between bullying and firm management". "Who will do the training?" asks Jane, to which Stan responds impatiently, "That's further down the line", almost imper-ceptibly turning to Trish from HR for reassurance. "But who selects the investigators?" asks Jane again, "The bullies?" "Of course not!" snaps Stan as he texts his PA to bring more Blu-Tack, a sure sign the brainstorming is going well; "It's open to everyone ... we will make sure of it in the job description ...". Stan muses momentarily about hierarchy and realises something is missing: "It makes sense for HR to manage the investigators don't you think?" Trish nods enthusiastically as the last hope of a meaningful consultation slips away. The meeting draws to a close with Stan lamenting the shortage of time, congratulating everyone on "The great work done today".

Bureaucracy is how we manage our lack of trust. From cradle to grave, the sophisticated mind-reading skills described by attachment behaviour helped us reach out and get the care we need to survive. When we cannot trust others to give us what we want when we need it, then we must have some kind of system to control people and resources. This goes some way to explaining the success of bureaucracies as an organising system. However, a tension exists between our skills in reading another's mind and our fear of communal life: being at the table or on the menu. In submitting to the control of others as a way of feeling secure, we must also sacrifice having our needs, wants, and hungers met by those who are too distant from us to care. This seems, for me, to be at the heart of our incongruence at work. A bureaucracy protects itself from being undermined by pathologising the individual worker. If I am ill, stressed, unhappy, despairing, angry, fearful, ashamed, the target of bullying, disengaged, or in need of discipline, then I have somehow brought it on myself. As individuals, we are left to wrestle with a problem that could not have arisen in isolation. Shopping, alcohol, medication, social media, food, intellectualising, and emotional aggression are all ways for us to avoid, withdraw, or dissociate from what we feel. The way forward has to be holistic (Fairfield, 2013).

Allowing learning and change to take place from the "ground up" as opposed to the "top down" requires a high degree of trust by organisational representatives because the reflections and conclusions of workers may not conform to what managers want to hear. Inviting managers to devolve creativity to the grass roots would be like asking the turkeys of Michels' *Iron Law* to vote for Thanksgiving/Christmas. Creative and congruent employees are more interested in being good at what they do, which may not always meet the criteria of managers who seek conformity and doing things correctly. If we wish to rise above the superficial problem-solving that seems only to happen under the pressure of a reductionist bureaucracy, reflexive learning consistent with the work of adolescence needs to take place at an organisational level.

Experimenting with alternatives. Organisations can become entrenched in a culture that limits growth. Experimenting with new ways of being is crucial to an organisation that is serious about remaining responsive and alive to its environment. In parallel with what works for an individual in counselling, it is vital that groups within an organisation are supported in having their voices heard and their needs met as part of a co-created, appreciative process. Sustainable change requires a holistic understanding of what the change means and feels like, so that ingrained thinking, behaviours, and actions can move aside for a different way of being. This requires an awareness of the subcultures that may block or get in the way of change. Although the individual has the benefit of a counsellor to support his or her awareness of configurations, the organising function of culture is usually out of awareness, or simply denied. Radical change must be explored through ring-fenced or localised experiments with a clearly defined team working in a safe, contained, and separate environment or "incubator" for letting go of the past and allowing workers to behave differently. In mirroring holistic *Appreciative Inquiry* (Chapter 2), it is important to resolve Erikson's crossroads of *trust* versus *mistrust* at an organisational level and recognise that workers are quick to adopt what seems to work. As I outlined in earlier chapters, when trusted, workers can seek out their own sources of support and wisdom in the context of their peers, groups, mentors, and supervisors.

It is time to trust *from the ground up*, and promote both *clan* and *development* cultures in our organisations. While I do not expect this to happen quickly though global emergencies appear to make it more likely, I hope you will hold onto this book, share its ideas, and perhaps when we come to our senses, use it to build a more compassionate workplace firmly anchored in the solid ground of a *Relational Approach*.

Things to keep in mind

- Bureaucratic structures exist to help us feel secure when we cannot *trust*. If we are serious about wellbeing, then conversations need to be about trust *versus* mistrust.
- Denying the invisible, blundering hand of the *market* requires that we put our *trust* in workers to solve the problems that affect them.
- Reflexive working pays attention to your life stage, which acknowledges your experience as a human being. Appraisals and professional development reviews must acknowledge this self-evident truth.
- Workers' rights to inalienable protections from their employers and the benefits of collective action are ideas that have been eroded in the past decades. It is time to leave your bubble and engage with people who are not like you. Join your union and become active in

changing the conversation. Do not wait for change to happen "one retirement at a time".

• If we can only learn to allow people to thrive, we will find that the plan for growth and development are already in place.

References

Business in the Community (2017). https://wellbeing.bitc.org.uk/sites/default/files/business_in_the_community_suicide_prevention_toolkit_0.pdf [Accessed 24.01.2019].

Baile WF, Buckman R, Lenzi R, Glober G, Beale EA, & Kudelka AP. (2000). SPIKES – A six-step protocol for delivering bad news: application to the patient with cancer. *The Oncologist*, 5, 302–311.

Dunn MG, Rochlen AB, & O'Brien KM. (2013). Employee, mother, and partner: An exploratory investigation of working women with stay-at-home fathers. *Journal of Career Development*, 40(1), 3–22.

Eriksen TE & Risør MB. (2014). What is called symptom? *Medical Health Care and Philosophy*, 17, 89–102.

Erikson EH. (1980). *Identity and the life cycle.* New York: Norton.

Fairfield M. (2013). The relational movement. *British Gestalt Journal*, 22(1), 22–35.

Finkelstein LM, Ryan KM, & King EB. (2013). What do the young (old) people think of me? Content and accuracy of age-based meta-stereotypes. *European Journal of Work and Organizational Psychology*, 22(6), 633–657.

Gartzia G, Sánchez-Vidal ME, & Cegarra-Leiva D. (2018). Male leaders with paternity leaves: Effects of work norms on effectiveness evaluations. *European Journal of Work and Organizational Psychology*, 27(6), 793–808.

Kerpelman JL & Pittman JF. (2018). Erikson and the relational context of identity: Strengthening connections with attachment theory. *Identity*, 18(4), 306–314.

Kirschenbaum H. (2007). *The Life and Works of Carl Rogers.* Monmouth: PCCS Books.

Klass D, Silverman PR, & Nickman SL. (1996). *Continuing bonds: New understandings of grief.* London: Taylor & Francis.

Miller T. (2011). Making sense of fatherhood: Gender, caring and work. Cambridge: Cambridge University Press.

Osborne JW. (2009). Commentary on retirement, identity, and Erikson's developmental stage model. *Canadian Journal on Aging*, 28(4), 295–301.

Skogstad M, Skorstad M, Lie A, Conradi HS, Heir T, & Weisæth L. (2013). Work-related post-traumatic stress disorder. *Occupational Medicine*, 63, 175–182.

Steinhauser KE, Alexander SC, Byock IR, George LK, & Tulsky JA. (2009). Seriously ill patients' discussions of preparation and life completion: An intervention to assist with transition at the end of life. *Palliative and Supportive Care*, 7, 393–404.

Terkel S. (1974). *Working.* London: Penguin.

Thompson N & Thompson S. (2009). Loss, grief and trauma. In N Thompson & J Bates (Eds.) *Promoting workplace well-being* (pp. 71–82). Basingstoke: Palgrave Macmillan.

Van der Kolk BE. (2006). Clinical implications of neuroscience research in PTSD. *Annals of the New York Academy of Sciences*, 1071, 277–293.

Vinten G & Lane DA. (2002). Counselling remaining employees in redundancy situations. *Career Development International*, 7(7), 430–437.

Final thoughts

This short book is by no means definitive and I am sure it will not be the last word on *Workplace Wellbeing*. I hope, however, that you will have found it a useful guide for reflecting on the values, attitudes, and practices of your workplace. Perhaps you, your colleagues, and your clients/customers/service users already flourish because you have adopted a *Relational Approach*? If not, then how sustainable is this for you? Like Cora in the Introduction, do you dream of another life? What I described earlier as a palliative approach to wellbeing encourages individuals to adapt to survive an environment that is emotionally harmful. The alternative stance of prevention that I have promoted here invites us to contemplate something more sustainable and ambitious, which is to challenge and ultimately modify the systems we use to organise our experience of work.

Although easily stated, a *Relational Approach* is challenging in practice, requiring time, patience, and the capacity to forgive ourselves for only being "good enough". It is not just about a collection of skills, but a set of attitudes which includes valuing being connected to others. Change in ourselves and for those around us begins with conversations, perhaps with friends, family, and trusted colleagues. Also remember that relationships and therefore conversations with those who are fondly or otherwise remembered continue even after they are gone. Their voices shape your attitudes, which includes whether you believe that your individual wellbeing is connected to that of the wider work community to which you belong. Your inalienable right to protection from your employer, and the benefits of collective action through unions and the like, are ideas that have fallen out of fashion in the past decades. Like a metal, which loses its strength and malleability as it passes from solid to vapour, so the atomised workplace reflects what happens to a community of workers when it is reduced to its individual parts.

I have argued that although rarely expressed, the modern workplace is increasingly about the exchange of your emotional labour for cash. Being a person and not a cog in a machine means a metaphorical line cannot be drawn around you and your work. This means we cannot hold our workplace wholly

Figure C.1 Pandora's Filing Cabinet.

responsible for whether we flourish, because the world of work merely amplifies the hypernormal assumptions, injustices, inequalities, and prejudices of its context. This sounds like a hopeless situation, and potentially lets organisations off the hook in their duty of care. This will only be true if we choose to see the bars of our invisible cage as being made of iron, as opposed to being gossamer threads. You begin to change the way things are done by engaging with and modelling a *Relational Approach* with every encounter. Just as "charity begins in the home", so we can transform the workplace by expecting to be met, and to see others holistically.

Because the workplace can trigger so much from our early family life, I brought to bear some well-established ideas and principles from psychodynamic and humanistic psychotherapy and integrated them into a *Relational Approach*. It is important to emphasise that I am not promoting some kind of homogenising brand. What is inspirational about adopting a *Relational Approach* is that you, as a unique human being, will co-create an equally unique relationship with each person you encounter. My integration of TA along with exercises in self-awareness acknowledges that relational competence is the keystone for change. It is functional, gloriously human relationships and not perfect ones that promote our sense of psychological wellbeing and personal growth.

In a world full of danger where survival was a matter of knowing who to trust, evolution selected for our capacity to dominate. The burgeoning of bureaucracy, with its pecking orders and mechanisms for command and control, seemed to be the answer to the problem of trusting others. Evolutionarily powerful emotions such as fear, shame, and anger, so central to the avoidance of danger, were filed away in Pandora's cabinet and denied through emergent processes. But the tremors of these denied emotions are felt throughout our organisations, and managed by phenomena like functional stupidity, the corruption complex, and when left unchecked, emotional abuse. Emergent behaviours seem to prevent us from thinking, feeling, and learning because we are seduced into avoiding emotions that are arguably no longer appropriate for sophisticated, reflective, social beings in the contexts we have created for ourselves. Reflexivity is the cornerstone of a *Relational Approach*, with the core conditions of empathy, authenticity, and acceptance serving to process emotions, rather than deny them. Organisations, particularly those engaged in emotionally challenging activities, who are serious about their workforce flourishing will privilege peer-to-peer influencing, supervision, and mentoring as practices that promote reflexivity. Emergence recognises that for any living system, be it a cell, group, organisation, or ecosystem, when an element fails to flourish, the wellbeing of the whole is impoverished, and vice versa. We can no longer afford to deny what lies in Pandora's filing cabinet, and I hope that I have convinced you that if an organisation can embody the core conditions of a *Relational Approach*, then the workplace becomes a less-risky place to bring our authentic selves.

The key argument throughout this book is that the values embodied in a *Relational Approach* can be successfully transported beyond the consulting room of the psychotherapist to other contexts. Any relationship based on exploitation and a disregard for the other is unsustainable. This means that relationships with family, friends, those we teach, along with the global challenges we face around conflict resolution, public health and climate change, can also benefit. This is because a *Relational Approach* invites us to know ourselves and our place in the family of things, which includes how, with whom, and where we live.

Index

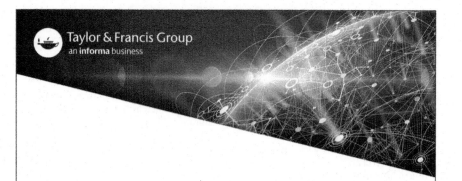